ANUNNAKI

Reptilians, History, Myths, Science and Humankind

(2 Books in 1)

by

Henry Krane

ANUNNAKI: Reptilians, History, Myths, Science, and Humankind (2 Books in 1)
Copyright © 2023 by Henry Krane
All rights reserved. ©2023, Henry Krane

Any reproduction, distribution, or public display, in whole or in part, without written permission from the copyright holders is strictly prohibited and may be subject to legal penalties under applicable laws. This includes photocopying, electronic processing, as well as the distribution of copies through rental or public lending.

EKR-19 EDITORIAL LLC Offices: 19 Liverpool Orange Avenue

Latest Edition: October 29th, 2022

1597 - United Kingdom

ANUNNAKI

Reptilians in the History of Humankind

by

HENRY KRANE

May the truth be your truth, reader.

The Reptile Gods

The most ancient civilization known to man is the Sumerian civilization. In their ancient writings, the Sumerians tell us about the existence of beings from outside this world, *who came from the stars.*

Ancient Sumeria flourished between 3000-2000 B.C. According to the translations of the Sumerian tablets by Zecharia Sitchin, a writer and expert in ancient languages, he informs us that in ancient Sumeria, there were beings called Anunnaki, which translates to *"The ones who came to Earth from the sky."* In his translations, Sitchin explains that these gods came from the stars and genetically modified Homo Erectus to create Homo Sapiens, meaning they created us.

However, what Zecharia Sitchin does not reveal is that these Anunnaki beings had a reptile form, with a humanoid body covered in scales. How do we know this? It's quite simple. The Sumerians left behind numerous clues about these beings, including thousands of representations found in paintings within their caves and stone statuettes created in their gods' likeness.

The Sumerians were the first to speak about the Anunnaki, but they were not the only civilization to reference these beings or gods.

In Mexico, thousands of kilometers away from the Sumerian culture and with a significant time difference of 3000 years, the ancient Maya worshipped a god known as Quetzalcóatl, the renowned feathered serpent.

Quetzalcóatl was one of the most prominent gods among the extensive pantheon worshipped by the Maya, and according to their beliefs, these gods also originated from the stars, aligning with the same notion as the Sumerians.

The name Quetzalcóatl is derived from two words: "Quetzal," which means "feather," and "cōātl," which means "serpent."

For the Maya culture and other folks like the Nahuátl, the brother of Quetzalcóatl was Tezcatlipoca, whose name means 'Black Smoking mirror.' Tezcatl means 'mirror,' tliltic means 'black,' and poctli means 'smoke.'

According to the Toltecs, these gods were rivals, similar to the gods Enki and Enlil of Sumerian culture, who were initially brothers and later became rivals. It is a significant coincidence between both cultures, which are greatly separated by time and distance.

These are two supreme gods from both Mesoamerican civilizations.

In the Toltec civilization, there existed a god called Gucumatz, described as "A Wisdom Serpent," who passed knowledge to humankind. Its Maya counterpart is believed to be Quetzalcóatl, and in Yucatán, this god was called Kukulcan.

Were Gucumatz, Quetzalcóatl, and Kukulkan the same Anunnaki god, Enki, who transmitted his knowledge to the Sumerians?

Another civilization that also worshipped these reptilian gods was the Inca civilization. They worshipped a god called Urcaguary, who was known as "The God of Subterranean Treasures." This god was represented as a huge reptile with a deer's head and used golden chains on its tail.

Urcaguary was considered as "The Divinity of what

was underground." The name itself recalls a Sumerian city called Ur. The name Urcaguary starts with "Ur," and many native people in the surrounding areas pronounce the name of this god as Ur-caguary. Another strange coincidence...

In North America, the Hopi Native Americans, located in Arizona, claim that their ancestors were visited by beings who traveled in large flying shields and, moreover, possessed the art of cutting and transporting large stone blocks, as well as constructing enormous and long tunnels and underground facilities.

The Hopi tribe refers to a race of reptilians living underground as "The Snake Brothers" and calls them Sheti. Similar to the Inca civilization, the Hopi tell us that these beings lived underground. Urcaguary lived underground as well.

And the coincidences continue in all these civilizations, despite being separated by gigantic distances of time and kilometers.

The Hopi also had a feathered serpent god called Baholinkonga, and the Native American culture is replete with serpents. Even the famous and mysterious mound with a serpent form can be found in the state of Ohio.

Now, in Asia, specifically in India, we discover that Hindu culture features beings known as Nagas, who are demigods with serpent forms.

In the epic text Mahabharata, written in the third century B.C., it is mentioned that the Nagas tend to be *negative beings* or *malevolent beings*. The text tells us that these Naga beings, known as *"The Hunters of all the Creatures,"* possess venomous poison, immense power, and excessive strength. They are always seeking to devour other creatures.

In the same continent, but 1500 years apart from Hindu mythology, we find Chinese mythology, which is known thanks to texts dating back to the Han Dynasty. This mythology speaks of its countless gods, such as Lóng Wáng, known as *"The Dragon King."*

Among the Chinese gods, we also have Fucanglong, who is referred to as *"The Dragon of the Lost Treasures"*; ShenLong, known as *"The Dragon of the Rain"*; and DinLong, known as *"The Dragon of the Earth."* The mythology is abundant with dragon gods, and if we infer, these dragons have reptilian forms. These beings are truly reptilian beings.

In the Oceanic Continent, within Australian mythology, we find The Rainbow Serpent, a being that holds an integral role in Aboriginal Australian culture. This serpent is associated with the *"Time of the Dream,"* a pre-human era in which the spirits shaped the *Physical World* and established its rules and laws.

The Rainbow Serpent is not considered a conventional god in Australian mythology, as gods, in the traditional sense, do not exist. However, it is a sacred being that is part of a vast collection of stories that form the foundation of Aboriginal spirituality.

Across these civilizations, regardless of time or distance, we observe a recurring theme: gods with reptilian forms that originate from the stars. This leads us to speculate that the Anunnaki gods, discussed by authors like Zecharia Sitchin (such as Anu, Enki, and Enlil), were not only worshipped in Sumeria. Due to their longevity and advanced technology, they could travel across the Earth and introduce different human races to various

8

continents, where civilizations were established to worship them from different parts of the world.

Undoubtedly, the Anunnaki imparted diverse languages to humankind as a means to divide them. Consequently, throughout history and across different civilizations, these gods (Anu, Enki, Enlil, Marduk, among others) were known by various names. But the question arises: why would the gods do such a thing?

Gave diverse languages to humans to divide them.

We Are Reptilians Food

These reptilian gods who coexisted with human beings, as the ancient Sumerian Tablets tell us, and as The Bible reaffirms in the Old Testament. What did these reptilian gods feed on? What did these reptilian gods eat...?

Well, these reptilian gods were in an evolutionary period, in which they were highly advanced and on the verge of transitioning to the fourth dimension... They were about to evolve.

These gods fed in two ways: through the consumption of food, just like us—meat from animals, vegetables and also human flesh...

...The other way, when these gods arrived on Earth, they had the capacity or began to develop the ability to feed on frequencies, through the energy we emit with our feelings, emotions, and thoughts. That is to say, these beings already had the ability to feed energetically.

That is why when they created the Sumerian civilization, the first human civilization, they realized that we could not only serve them as slaves, but these gods also realized that we could serve them as food. Energy food.

There are many, many researchers who come to this conclusion. Such is the case of David Icke in his books: *The Robots' Rebellion* (1994), *And the Truth Shall Set You Free* (1995), *The Biggest Secret* (1999), *and Children of the Matrix* (2001).

Carlos Castañeda refers to these beings as *"The Predators of Humankind"*. Gnostics claim that the Archons feed from us.

Among all these researchers, the one who comes closest to the truth, the one who has been more accurate than anyone else regarding the Anunnaki, is Salvador Freixedo. His investigations leave no doubt in his books and provide us with real evidence that there are gods who feed on us.

But how do we know this is real? What do these researchers base their conclusions on regarding these beings feeding on our bodies and energies, such as our feelings and thoughts?

To answer this, we will begin analyzing the evidence left throughout human history. We will see that within it, there is ample demonstration that this is a very, very real possibility.

To begin with, we must understand that our ancestors were not crazy, much less barbarians, as our teachers of the System in this Matrix in which we live each of our days want us to believe in schools. Our ancestors were intelligent beings with advanced knowledge in Mathematics, Astronomy, and Architecture. For example, the pyramids of Egypt, which would be almost impossible to replicate today despite all the technology we have. Archaeology itself has demonstrated this.

But if our ancestors were so intelligent and advanced, why on earth did they carry out human sacrifices? Why did they perform them?

The answer is simple: the gods manipulated all ancient civilizations, making them believe that if they didn't perform these sacrifices, they would cause catastrophes, destroy cities, and bring about many other natural phenomena that they were capable of producing.

The condition was simple: either there were sacrifices or everyone would be destroyed.

These gods fed on the low frequencies that were generated when we died or when we were afraid, and they greatly enjoyed the emanations from our burnt flesh. Furthermore, as I mentioned before, some of these gods and their hybrids (half human, half reptile) - who were the high priests and kings that ruled the ancient civilizations - drank the blood and ate the human flesh of our ancestors.

Now, understanding the above, especially the fact that our ancestors were not crazy or mere barbarians, but rather possessed intelligence similar to ours. The only thing that differentiated us was that they had access to godly technology, which they did not fully comprehend. However, nowadays, we can understand the nature of technology itself: how a computer works, how an airplane flies. We have only just begun to understand it...

Now, let us see all the human sacrifices that have been done in the name of these gods through history.

Let us start with the most ancient civilization, the Sumerian. In which shepherds, to please their gods, sacrificed their animals burning them, reaching to them the perfumed smoke. That tell us the Sumerian Tablets.

After that, at some point, the reptile gods realized they did not only like the smell of burnt meat, but also the smell and taste of burnt human flesh.

In Mexico, the Aztec made human sacrifices for the Sun not to turn off. For them, the blood was a source of sacred life, and it was offered to the god Huitzilopochtli. This civilization was quite brutal with the sacrifices of their captured enemies as well as with those of the volunteer folks.

Historians say that the humans offered as sacrifice had to climb to the top of the pyramid and there a priest cut them from the throat to the stomach in order to take their heart out and then give it to Huitzilopochtli.

Mayas performed sacrifices too. In order to do that, they played cosmogonic myths, which had an important religious and ideological meaning; something clearly seen in their famous ball game at which the losers where sacrificed to Quetzalcóatl.

In Peru the Incas, to avoid natural disaster, made sacrifices and offered them to their gods. Usually, they sacrificed prisoners and children who were raised for this dark purpose: To be sacrificed to their gods.

Celts were known for making human sacrifices for religion. They were always guided by a druid *(a man with authority and who, among Gaelic and Celt folks, could play priest, teacher, judge and also public administrator)*. The sacrifice consisted on burying a blade at a man's back and watching how he moved until death. These spasms were considered as gods' prophecies.

Also, the millenary Chinese culture was marked by human sacrifices for many dynasties, especially at Shang Dynasty time.

Chinese practiced three types of sacrifice: the first one was the pit, where young men were sacrificed: they were replanted, and buried without their material belongings — they were buried alive; the second one was the institution where children and babies were violently sacrificed with no material belongings; the third one was confining, where little girls were sacrificed to be buried after that according to the ritual.

One of the most ancient and interesting civilizations is

the Carthaginians, who performed human sacrifices out of two reasons: the favor of the gods, and population control. They sacrificed the newborns. It is believed that between 800 – 146 B.C, this civilization sacrificed 2000 babies.

It is also worthy to mention the Hindu civilization. They venerated, with sacrifices, the goddess Shakti, and in Bengal, these sacrifices were practiced until XIX century.

It is unbelievable how these gods manipulated all these ancient civilizations. However, this does not end here. One of the books that clearly show us how the gods demanded human sacrifices since the beginning of the times is The Bible. And we see how in the Old Testament, Yahweh, this god, self-called the only god and creator of humankind, demanded sacrifices to ease his anger.

For example, we read at JUDGES 11:31: *"Whatever comes out of the home of my house to meet me when I return in triumph from the Ammonites will be the LORD's and I will sacrifice it as a holocaust."*

Well, holocaust comes from the Latin *holocaustum*. And, according to the Israelites, it means: "sacrifice at which the victim is completely burnt."

In another biblical cite, we can read: *"And Jehovah said to Moses: Take all the princes of these people and hang them before Jehovah, in front of the Sun and Jehovah's anger will turn away from Israel"* —Numbers 25:4.

In Exodus 13:1, 2: *"Jehovah said to Moses: Consecrate to me every firstborn male. The firstborn from every womb among the Israelites belongs to me, both of man and beast."*

In order to understand this verse, we have to know what consecrate means. According to the definition, it means: Dedicate or grant a person or other thing to God as a cult or vow.

We also read in Exodus 22:29, 30: *"You shall not delay the news of your harvest nor winery, you shall offer me the firstborn of your sons. You shall do the same with your ox's and sheep's firstborns. For seven days he will be with his mother and at the eighth day you will offer him to me."*

It is clear that this god Jehovah was the very same God Enlil. We will see it later.

In Greece, in the Greek mythology, offerings and sacrifices were made in the name of the gods to gain their favors. We have, for example, in the story of the Minotaur, that the Athens sent fourteen young people to feed the beast.

At the beginning of the Roman Republic, the people who broke their promises and tricked others were offered as sacrifice to their gods.

Romans offered war prisoners and virgins to their gods. Also, in the Roman Empire, the popular custom of killing sons, called filicide, was related to the *patria potestas*, which allowed paterfamilias to sell, kill, offer to the gods, subordinate into any activity, and devour the sons.

According to Plinio *"The Old,"* human sacrifices were abolished by a senatorial command in the year 97 B.C. and the Roman Empire forbade these acts calling them barbarian.

But, really do all these sacrifices end here? Does the story of human sacrifice end with this prohibition of Rome? Anyone would say yes. Well, this is not entirely true...

Human sacrifices were changed for gladiator fights. They camouflaged these human sacrifices turning them into a show for all the people, but no one protested and no one considered it as a barbaric act.

This is how the gods camouflaged these human sacrifices, and nowadays they are still carried out, but with other names: the Holy Inquisition, the Crusades, the First and Second World War, the false aerial accidents like the one of Germanwings, or like the hijacked plane in Malaysia, or the Twin Towers attack, etc.

But in this "Accident" at the Twin Towers, specifically, such was the ritual that we can even see the faces of these demons in the smoke of the Twin Towers burning, the faces of these reptilian gods that begin to materialize in this third dimension. It was so much the energy these beings got from the burning human flesh that these gods began to materialize.

Also, the so-called aerial "accidents" like that of Germanwings are considered human sacrifices. This does not mean all accidents that occur are considered sacrifices for these gods. However, those that are made on ritual dates, and those that are very noisy, should be considered as planned for these gods to be fed.

At present time there are many clues of these sacrifices still being made. For example, the satanic sacrifices performed to be able to communicate with these demons, which actually are these reptilian gods. And this is endorsed by the millions and millions of people who have disappeared worldwide, year after year, women and children included. Where are all of these people going? Well, obviously they are sacrifices this elite performs. Although it is hard to believe, it is the reality...

Reptilians fed on the energy of the dying on 9/11

Sacrifices

Dinosaurs Extinction and the War between Two Races

Sixty-five million years ago, there was a war between the Reptilians coming from the constellation of Orion and the Lyrans from the constellation of Lyra. This war lasted many years, and in one of the battles in which the Vegans (from the star Vega, which is in the constellation of Lyra), who had made an alliance with the Lyrans to put an end to the Reptilians, were fighting, they decided to flee and discovered a planet. That planet was Earth.

These Vegans landed on Earth. They decided to hide in it from the Reptilians. Obviously, the Reptilians found them, they decided to attack them with nuclear technology, while the vegans decided to counterattack with their last nuclear weapons of their last remaining ships, producing then this Great War on Earth.

In those times the dinosaurs already existed.

When the Galactic Confederation realized that the vegans and Reptilians were using nuclear weapons on the virgin planet called Earth, which they were observing and guarding their evolution, they decided to intervene. They sent two of their most powerful races: the Carians and the Felines, with the only mission of safeguarding as much life as possible existing on Earth so the living beings there could continue evolving.

Upon arriving on Earth, the Carians decided to save the dinosaurs by moving them, guiding them to the Abzu (the interior of the planet Earth). While the Felines guarded the entrances of the North Pole and South Pole. In this way, they managed to save a lot of dinosaurs. Although many of the dinosaur species were not saved due to the number of nuclear weapons used in this war, most of the dinosaur species were saved in the Abzu, in the interior of the Earth.

Interestingly, the Carians and Felines also saved a very primitive race of human beings. Some of us were hidden in the Abzu, while others were saved in the caverns. That is how it was possible to save a large number of living beings on Earth.

The Felines, when this battle was over, gave an ultimatum to the Reptilians to move away from the planet Earth. Otherwise, they would have problems with that race, the only one capable of facing them.

The few Reptilians left alive withdrew when they won the battle. That is how it was possible to save as many species of dinosaurs on Earth.

What they tell us in school about the dinosaurs that became extinct due to a huge meteorite is false. They continue to live in the Abzu, inside the Earth...

At the end of this great war of Orion and the Reptilians being victorious, the Galactic Confederation decided that the Carians would take over the safety of planet Earth. But the Carians, living so long with the dinosaurs in the Abzu, decided to modify them genetically to accelerate their evolution, being born then a new reptilian sub-race. That is how the first race with intelligence started.

Humans were not the first to evolve and have intelligence. It was this new reptilian race that takes us millions of years of advantage in technology and

intelligence and that is within the depths of the Earth.
However, this is not the only intelligent race...

The Creation of the Giants and the Man

The Carians passed on their knowledge to their new creation, this new reptilian race. It is there where the construction of new civilizations started, in the entrances of the Abzu. Meanwhile, on the surface of the Earth, the hominids began to evolve slowly. This is how four million years ago, approximately, the Carians decided to abandon and grant the planet to the Galactic Confederation, leaving these Reptilians very advanced both technologically and spiritually.

This reptilian race —Intraterrestrials or Intraterrestrial Reptilians— considered the Carians as their guides and creators.

Very rarely Intraterrestrials came to the surface of the Earth. This was because they did not like the surface climate. They were already completely adapted to the warm and constant climate they had inside the Abzu.

This race came to the surface only for the purpose of scientific research to study the various species that existed in it. There they realized that the hominids had many signals of intelligence; more than the rest of the species that existed on the planet. It was a really accelerated evolution, which they began to study more closely.

For a long time, four hundred thousand years ago approximately, a mother ship from Orion arrived to the Earth with over four hundred Reptilians and two hundred grey ones beings *(the grey ones)* —this last race, according to the Sumerian tablets, was called as The Igigi—. These two races came to Earth on their mother ship because they were escaping from an intergalactic war. They were looking for a refuge, in this case, a planet, with enough natural resources to survive.

It should be noted that this race that came to Earth was not a pure race of Reptilians who time ago, once came to our planet, but was a sub-race, a secondary race of these Reptilians from Orion.

Anu was the chief commander, and his two sons, Enki and Enlil, were the sub-heads of the reptilian caravan that had arrived on Earth. Both brothers were always in a very tough competition to see which of the two would be the heir to the throne since Anu was the king and boss of this sub-race.

When they arrived, they decided to build a settlement and create a dimensional portal to communicate with their planet. And for this, they decided to redirect the causes of the river Euphrates and Tigris. And they also began to extract the natural resources of our planet, and many minerals, especially, gold.

All the heavy mining, construction, and mining tasks were entrusted to the Igigi. But these Reptilians did not count on them, at some point, rebelling against the construction of this portal and extraction of minerals, so these Reptilians summoned an Assembly; and it is at this point when Enki convinces his father, Anu, and the entire Anunnaki Council, to create a Lulu, that is, a slave.

Enki had realized that there was a primitive being, which denoted and gave signs of primitive intelligence. He was the one who had the idea of genetically modifying that primitive being. All of this was done to be able to replace the grey ones with these new slaves.

Meanwhile, the Intraterrestrials had not realized that these beings from Orion had already arrived on our planet. It was not until much later that they realized that there was already a race that had begun to manipulate Homo erectus genetically, until these new visitors started doing these experiments, and creating technology on the surface of the Earth. Therefore, these Intraterrestrial beings decided to appear before this caravan and realized that these Orion beings were very few.

In the interview with Anu, they came to an agreement: that the visiting Reptilians would not intervene in the depths of the Abzu, that they would not extract the natural resources from the interior of the Earth. While the Intraterrestrials would allow them to finish the portal so they can communicate to their planet and be able to return to it.

But this was a deal with which Anu cheated to the intraterrestrial beings. Anu felt afraid because in reality he was outnumbered. In addition, they did not have many weapons to fight against the Intraterrestrials. But being both reptilian races, they decided to share their knowledge and technology. This is how they began to build their settlements much faster.

In this same period of time, the Galactic Confederation detected the mothership on the surface of the Earth. Then they decided to send a group of Carians and see what kind of plans these reptilian beings had.

Upon arriving on Earth, the Carians realized that the Intraterrestrials —Their creation— were already collaborating with this race from Orion, so they decided to meet with Anu to know the plans of his race, so Anu once more resorted to lie indicating that he was going to build a portal to be able to communicate with his planet and return to it once the war was over.

Anu knew that in reality, the Galactic Confederation did not have enough resources to take care of them on planet Earth because they were investing them in the war. The Carians also knew it, so they decided to stay and watch over these visiting Reptilians.

After several attempts and failures of Enki at creating monsters and beings without enough intelligence to do the tasks that his race needed and that the grey ones had refused so much to do, he was about to abandon the project because he could not find the exit from his labyrinth that he had engineered himself.

Because of that, the Carians decided to help Enki by transmitting their knowledge and technology on how they had managed to evolve the dinosaurs quickly. It was the Carians who gave the clue to Enki to accelerate the evolution of the hominids.

They revealed to him that it was not enough to mix a reptilian ovule and a hominid sperm, but he needed to mix many more characteristics of other extraterrestrial races. The Carians gave him their genes as well as the race of Intraterrestrials. Meanwhile, Enki also had a gene bank of the races he had collected. In total there were 23 genes from different races of the whole universe that were mixed in a great genetic cocktail. They also told Enki that man's semen should be implanted in a reptilian uterus. That is how the Homo sapiens was born, a being with the intelligence and sufficient strength to perform the tasks they needed: a perfect Lulu. HOMO SAPIENS

However, if this Lulu was created, where are the giants? Did they really exist?

To answer these questions, we have to resort to two theories: the first, tells us that these Lulus, were not fast nor even strong enough to build at the pace that the Reptilians required, so Enki was entrusted once more to take over the genetic modification, and his idea for this was that we reproduced faster, because he thought that having a very large workforce, they would finish the portal in a very short time, something that is not common in nature. This is the explanation that we humans are always in heat.

»He did this with a double sense, obviously in the eyes of Anu and the Anunnaki Council, this was for the workforce to grow more numerous, but in reality, Enki did it so that his creation would survive through time and would not be mere slaves. But this did not work. Being more numerous, men were actually not moving faster than what was required. Enki decided to create a being similar to Homo sapiens but bigger, stronger and faster. This is the first theory.

The second was: that these reptilian beings began to cross and have sex with Homo sapiens, human women. From this crossbreeding, appeared the giants we know, such as what explain many passages of the Bible in the Genesis…

The Extinction of Atlantis and Lemuria

The first human, the first Lulu, the first Homo sapiens that Enki created was called Adapa (according to the Sumerian Tablets). In Christian religion, it would be called Adan.

Later he created the first woman, Lilith (according to Sumerian tablets), the Biblical Eve. And these two human beings, by a decision of the Anunnaki Council, were taken to the mother ship. A very important fact to keep in mind is that the Anunnaki and the grey ones, but especially the first, physiologically did not adapt very well to the density of the Earth. They got suffocated quickly. After three to seven days on the surface, they began to feel discomfort. It is for this reason that the grey ones rebelled against such conditions and submission to this forced labor on the surface of the Earth.

The Reptilians decided to park their mother base in the orbit of the Earth. And they only went down to refuel, that is, for water.

Anu spent most of the time on the ship and rarely went down to Earth, while Enki, Enlil, and some other Reptilians did it.

Adapa and Lilith had a privileged treat from the Anunnaki since Anu and the Anunnaki Council really wanted the pure blood of these first Homo sapiens to prevail.

The plan was that the descendants of these were created through artificial matrices so that the purity of the blood would be one hundred percent. However, Enki at the first opportunity he had, confessed to Eva that they were free beings and that they could become like gods; that they could get to experience their emotions. That is when Eva (Lilith) knows the truth and convinces Adan (Adapa) to have sex.

Anu realized that they had disobeyed his orders and decides to punish them by returning them back to Earth, entrusting Enlil to watch over his ancestry to be the purest blood on Earth.

Enki, on the other hand, had already created women and men to begin to populate the Earth. This first race of Homo sapiens was very intelligent and had highly developed psychic abilities. Unlike us, they had more activated codons in their DNA. Of the 64, 32 were active, with which, they learned more quickly. But this was not what surprised the most the Reptilians. What surprised them the most of Homo sapiens was their ability to feel and express their feelings. Something that very few reptilian races had.

The plan continued their course and these Homo sapiens continued to be used as Lulu slaves to continue the works that the Igigi had left unfinished.

The reptilian Anunnaki commissioned the Igigi, the grey ones, to supervise the works. That is why they received the name of "Those who watch and observe" (according to Sumerian tablets).

The Anunnaki soon realized that when humans were exalted or suffering, when they expressed their feelings and emotions in a euphoric way, individually or as a group, they emanated subtle vibrations that were detected by the Anunnaki, and that caused them immense pleasure *(See*

26

Chapter 2, to understand more).

Initially, the Anunnaki and the Igigi transmitted much of their knowledge in Engineering, Agriculture, Astronomy, and Construction to humans so that they could learn and perform their tasks more quickly.

But Enlil realized about the danger of humans not being any kind of beings, because apparently, they were too intelligent and could rebel at any moment, so he decided to communicate this problem to Anu. They decided to create a system of beliefs in which humans should worship their gods. For this to be effective, Enlil began to manipulate them through fear, demonstrating miracles through technology that only the gods could do. It is at this point that they began to perform the sacrifices demanded by the gods to appease their anger.

Anu also strictly prohibited the Anunnaki to transmit the knowledge of technology or spirituality to human beings under very severe condemnations to anyone who dared to help them, even to death, to which Enki flatly opposed. He wanted his creation to be a free race, capable of evolving and developing self-awareness.

Enki was frustrated to see how his huge creation was being wasted on slaves performing heavy tasks, and despite that potential, they were also being manipulated so that they did not exploit the full potential they could reach. So, it occurred to him an idea for his creation to be able to develop. He told Anu that they should have a group of Lulus on another side, far from the Euphrates River, the first Anunnaki settlement, where all the created humans were concentrated, and who lived unnoticed by the watchful eyes of the Carians with the purpose of creating weapons and being prepared for some treachery or attack of the Intraterrestrials.

Anu agreed. But on a condition: Enki had to create a different race of Lulus, much stronger, and that they were disconnected more codons of their DNA to reduce their psychic capacity and their ability to procreate. Enki accepted. He created the second race of human beings, with black skin to resist the sun, and stronger physically, in return they lost their psychic abilities. They were employed as slaves for the arduous tasks, that the Anunnaki had.

Upon finishing his new creation, Enki went to Mu, a continent that was located in the Pacific Ocean, on the supposed secret mission of building weapons. With all the freedom of the world in this continent, Enki created the third race of humans, physically very similar to those of the first race, with the same psychic abilities, but only different in stature; since this third race, which was named Lemurians, had an average height of 2 to 2.5 meters in height.

Enki knew very well that the Anunnaki were going to want to visit the place where he was creating weapons, so he decided to move to the Atlantic having finished creating the Lemurians. The Atlantis, a huge continent located in the Atlantic Ocean. There he created the fourth race of humans, which had a similar physical aspect to those of the first race, of the same size and with the same physical capacities. The only difference is that they had a dark complexion and were much more intelligent. This race was called the Atlanteans.

To these two new races, all reptilian Anunnaki knowledge was revealed. From the construction of buildings through stones to the channeling of energy through the chakras.

No wonder that after a hundred years of civilization, these two races had already created great civilizations. But the Atlanteans did create atomic weapons and weapons that threw rays through crystals, prisms, and quartz, unlike the Lemurians who did not have any weapons.

These two great civilizations had large maritime ships and ships that could sail the sky. That is why the Lemurians could explore what we all know today as South Africa, Madagascar, Sri Lanka, Sumatra, Indian Ocean, Australia, and New Zealand. On the other hand, the Atlanteans managed to explore almost all the oceans existing in the world.

In all this time, Enki was showing several times the weapons created to Anu. He told him that he was hiding them somewhere in the Atlantic continent, that when they had a sufficient number he would tell him to finish the mission.

Meanwhile, in the first Anunnaki settlement, the Igigi were already considered the lesser gods. Their supervision tasks were entrusted to the first human race created by Enki. The heavy construction work was entrusted to the black race, the second created human race.

Now, picking up the line of investigation *(as mentioned in Chapter 4)*, that the giants were hybrid beings, in that same time, many reptilian beings had sexual relations with human women, creating so the giants and other various hybrids.

It is worth mentioning that not all reptilian and human children were giants. Some came out in their crosses of normal height. And these, obviously, were named as kings

29

and they did not have to worry about working. At this point, the clever human women began to extract the most valuable information from these reptilian beings with whom they copulated, about the knowledge that they were forbidden to reveal to Homo Sapiens.

Enlil, intoxicated by ego for the devotion that humans had towards their reptilian gods, put on test to a man descendant of Adapa that he chose to test his faith to him. This man named Abraham in the Bible was put on test many times. In one of them, Enlil, orders him to be circumcised along with his offspring. This must be transmitted from generation to generation so that he would know who his *chosen people* were. That is how Enlil's plan to be the only god on planet Earth started.

After a while, Enlil found out that some reptilian beings had violated the order not to offer knowledge to humans. These beings are named in the Bible as *"The Watchers"*, the famous *fallen angels* —do not confuse these beings with the Igigi, grey ones—. And to implant fear in humankind, Enlil chose Abraham's grandson, Enoch, to take him to his ship and show him the tortures practiced on these fallen angels for transmitting knowledge forbidden to humans. And entrusted him to transmit what he had seen for letting men and women know what awaited them if they broke the law again.

Twelve thousand years ago, approximately, Enlil decided to visit the Atlantic without notifying Enki. He was surprised by the advanced culture and technology this civilization had, apart from the weapons they had. Enlil went to his father, Anu and the Anunnaki council to inform them about Enki's treason. There, Enki admitted he put on test an improved human race to know how far they were able to get. He explained that his main mission was to create weapons and have them available for the Anunnaki Reptilians and that he had achieved that. In addition, he told them that the weapons were available for reptilian subjects, and he convinced them that this new breed could help them create new motherships and create new portals not only to communicate with Orion but also with other reptilian Anunnaki settlements.

Although Anu and the Anunnaki Council were not very convinced of this, at the end they gave their vote in favor, that this human race of Lulus would help them to create technology, but on the condition that they were watched by the Reptilians and that the weapons were transferred to the mother ship.

Faced with this decision, Enlil played his last card to destroy this advanced human race, since for him they were a danger, because they were not controlled or subdued like the human beings who were in the first settlement. He decided to give an order to one of his subjects to contact Intraterrestrials to inform them that the Anunnaki had created weapons to destroy them. In addition to tell them where these weapons were, and warn them to act fast, because the Anunnaki would soon transfer such weapons to the mothership to attack them.

The Intraterrestrial beings immediately notified the Carians and prepared for war. They sent an emissary to get in touch with Anu and inform him to abstain from that plan. When Anu received the emissary, he had no choice but to assume the creation of weapons, but he told them that in fact, these, were not to attack their allies, but were to take them to a reptilian base located in the Pleiades, that he did not want any war.

The Carians, on the other hand, also threatened Anu by telling him that, if they provoked a war, the Galactic Confederation would intervene to exterminate them or at least to expel them from the planet Earth.

Anu gave the same explanation to the Carians telling them not to misunderstand their intentions that he himself would order to destroy all those weapons.

The Intraterrestrials, on the other hand, had already discovered Mu and the Lemurians, and they also questioned the intention of creating such an advanced human civilization, to which Anu answered that he did not know the existence of this civilization.

The Carians also demanded the Anunnaki to destroy the portal they had created in the first settlement, to which Anu agreed.

Enlil, who already knew exactly what was going to happen, told Ziusudra, known as Noah in the Bible, who was the great-grandson of Enoch, to build a boat to save his lineage, since there was going to be a Universal Flood, and that the gods, Anu and Enlil, had decided it.

Anu gave the order to Enki to take the Carians and Intraterrestrials to the place of arms to supervise their disarmament. And another caravan of Intraterrestrials went to Lemuria and the first Anunnaki settlement to check that there were no more weapons.

Enlil had the mission to destroy the first portal created in the first settlement. Once the disarmament was finished, Enki realized that three nuclear weapons were missing, and he was questioned by the Intraterrestrials and the Carians about this.

Foreseeing what was going to happen, Enki sent a large part of the Atlanteans to take refuge in a boat and to sail to the sea. He did exactly the same with the Lemurians, putting them on a large ship.

Enlil, who stole these three weapons buried them close to human settlements: one in the Atlantic Ocean near Atlantis, another in the Persian Gulf near the first Anunnaki settlement, and another in the Pacific Ocean near Mu.

Once finished the boat of Ziusudra, Enlil activated these weapons causing three large tsunamis that caused the collapse of Atlantis, the disappearance almost completely of Mu, and the destruction of the first settlement next to the portal they had created.

The Universal Flood had begun with the annihilation of most of the human race and giant hybrids.

The Atlantean vessel was directed to America, the Lemurian vessel was directed to Asia, and the Ziuzudra ship to Europe, using the Black Sea...

The True Origin of the Moon

These civilizations being annihilated, the annoyed Carians told Anu that his race had violated one of the universal laws, for causing the extinction of a race. Anu answered them that the human race belonged to them because they had created it.

Enlil cleverly interrupted this discussion of Anu and the Carians by informing them that not all the human race had been extinguished. Since he had saved a handful of people who were on a small boat. In addition, there were survivors in the first settlement. Enki, who had been listening to all this conversation with the Carians, decided to keep quiet and say nothing about the Atlanteans and Lemurians that he had put safely on the boats.

The Carians questioned Enlil about why the humans were on that boat, they asked him if he already knew that these bombs were going to explode. To which Enlil replied that he had sent a group of Lulus on a boat to explore the area, which we now know as the border of Bulgaria and Romania since they had discovered a large gold deposit that he wanted to exploit. The Carians were not very convinced with Enlil's answer and they asked Anu why they had activated those three nuclear weapons. To which Anu, a bit calmer, told them that he did not know who had activated them, but had the suspicion of who they could have been, promising to carry out an investigation to get the responsible for all this to pay for their actions.

The Carians left the mother ship and went to what was left of the first settlement, accounting for ninety-three surviving humans, of which seven were hybrids (half human, half reptilian); no giants.

Once this was done, the Carians gave notice to the Galactic Confederation about the violation of the law that, in their judgment, the Anunnaki had made.

The Earth was in its lowest duration recorded in its history, all because of the explosion of these nuclear weapons.

The Intraterrestrials baffled and surprised by the destructive capacity of the Anunnaki, saw the perfect opportunity to attack and destroy them as they represented a great threat to them. However, they had a great disadvantage: despite having a large number of warriors, they did not have enough technology to reach the mother ship from Earth. His plan was to hijack the transporter ships to get to the mother ship and from there to destroy it from the inside. However, foreseeing all this, Anu approached to the intraterrestrial leaders and made a deal with them: the Anunnaki were going to teach the Intraterrestrials how to build weapons and sophisticated means of transport, as well as give them a good number of humans to help them in their manufacture.

The Intraterrestrials baffled and surprised by the destructive capacity of the Anunnaki, saw the perfect opportunity to attack and destroy them as they represented a great threat to them. However, they had a great disadvantage: despite having a large number of warriors, they did not have enough technology to reach the mother ship from Earth. His plan was to hijack the transporter ships to get to the mother ship and from there to destroy it from the inside. However, foreseeing all this, Anu approached to the intraterrestrial leaders and made a deal with them: the Anunnaki were going to teach the Intraterrestrials how to build weapons and sophisticated means of transport, as well as give them a good number of humans to help them in their manufacture.

The Intraterrestrials were in a great dilemma, because on the one hand, if they accepted the deal, their civilization would make a huge, evolutionary, and technological leap. But on the other hand, they were afraid that the Anunnaki would recreate new humans, Lulus, and begin to make weapons again, being a threat again for them.

In the end, the Intraterrestrials accepted this deal, but on two more conditions: the first was that no Anunnaki would enter the Abzu without their consent, and the second is that they also taught them the secrets of the genetic manipulation so that they could master it. Anu had no other option but to accept the terms of the Intraterrestrials in exchange for not attacking their race.

While this negotiation was being carried out, Anu ordered Enki the construction of seven hundred humans to repopulate the Earth. But this time, these humans would have only twenty active codons out of the sixty-four available in their DNA. This would be the fifth race of humans but no longer as intelligent as their ancestors nor with their psychic powers. In other words, he ordered to create the perfect Lulu.

Enki had no other choice and he accepted since he was being watched at all times by the Anunnaki on Anu's request since he did not want him to recreate humans as

36

ENKI WAS THE LEAST BAD REPTILIAN

intellectually powerful as he had done. The only hope of Enki was the Atlanteans and Lemurians that he had managed to rescue.

It is compelling to make a comment about Enki. It is not that he felt precisely love or any other kind of feeling benevolent to humans since reptilian beings did not have that kind of feelings because of their physiological nature. He felt pride and appreciation for his creation and did not want anyone to destroy it. He was not good, but he was the least bad of all the Anunnaki. He was supporting us to know how far we could get. He saw us as we currently see our pets.

Before anything, he was an Anunnaki, and he would always watch first for the benefits of his race rather than for us humans.

Having clarified this, we have that the Galactic Confederation, upon receiving the news of what had happened on Earth, asked the Draconians, the supreme race of all Reptilians, an explanation of what had happened. For if the Anunnaki Reptilians had destroyed a whole race consciously, it implied a violation of one of the universal laws.

The Draconians, surprised by this news, knew very well that if the Anunnaki had committed such an atrocity, the Kadistu could intervene and they would end up paying a very high price for this. They sent their emissaries to Anu demanding that he showed up in Orion so that he could give an explanation of this serious accusation.

When the Draconians came for Anu, he asked Enki to accompany him along with three other members of the Anunnaki Council and he commissioned the leadership of the Earth to Enlil.

Enki, did not feel supported by other Anunnaki, so he commanded the only one he trusted, his son Marduk, to watch over Enlil and not allow him to destroy humans. In addition, he entrusted him with the supervision of the remaining Lulus, since they had only created two hundred of the seven hundred that Anu had requested.

When arriving in Orion, Anu, head of the Anunnaki caravan, belonging to the Usumgal race, was interviewed by the Draconian leaders demanding an explanation of why they were not noticed of the planet found and the race of Lulus. Anu told them that he tried to build a portal to be able to communicate with all the Reptilian Alliance, but he could not do it. He also confirmed them that the Galactic Confederation was already aware of what they were doing and that even the Carians kept an eye on them.

The Draconians realized that if the rest of the Reptilian Alliance, of which they were also members, were not warned about this Anunnaki settlement, the rest of the reptilian races would come into conflict and would be jealous and desiring to take control of the new planet.

At last, Anu also confessed that the human race had the capacity to feed them with their subtle energy, provoking them an indescribable sensation.

The Draconians, subduing and threatening Anu, told him that from that moment on, the planet Uras (which is how they called the Earth) belonged to them along with the human Lulus. In addition, he was strictly forbidden to inform his Usumgal race and the Reptilian Alliance about this planet.

Anu, fearing for his life, accepted all the conditions of the Draconians, becoming from that moment on their slave.

Seven draconian days after having made the deal with the Draconians, the Galactic Confederation called to a first meeting to deal with the issue of the planet Uras, Earth, and the Lulus. The Galactic Confederation Council (GCC) met in the extinct planet Mulge, and to the venue arrived Anu and Enki, next to the three members of the Anunnaki Council.

The first question to Anu was why they did not inform the rest of the genetic manipulation they did to an inferior race, found on a planet outside their jurisdiction. Anu answered that the communication systems of his ship were rendered useless and that on the planet Uras, Earth, there were not the necessary elements to repair them, but what he was trying to do was to create a portal to notify the Reptilian Alliance of their position, but in the end, they were not successful either.

The Carians, members of the Galactic Confederation, told him that this was inadmissible. Making the decision to alter and accelerate the evolution of a race, interrupting it from its natural course was against the laws set forth in the Intergovernmental Treaties. The Draconians, who were the representatives of the reptilian race in the Galactic Confederation, interrupted their fellow Carians and told them that their emissaries had helped create the Lulus, and questioned why when they were notified that a reptilian race had manipulated an inferior race on the planet Uras, they did not decide to notify the Draconians, but on the contrary, they decided to be silent and send emissaries behind their backs without asking for authorization. That was also a violation of the Intergovernmental Treaties.

The angry Carians answered that they only wanted to

be sure and corroborate the information they received. And if they decided not to inform the Confederation, it was because they had more important problems to attend to because of the war that the Reptilians had caused.

After a long discussion, they came to the first agreement, that is: not to inform the Reptilian Alliance, and in general, to all the reptilian races of the birth of this new self-aware species of human Lulus and that inhabited the planet Uras, Earth, because if they did it, it could create a conflict in the interests of the rest of the reptilian races.

The Draconians voted in favor of this first agreement since it was very convenient for them to convert the Earth into one more of their *farms*, so they swore to respect this agreement with the rest of the Confederation.

The next question they asked Anu was why they had decided to accelerate the evolution of an inferior race, and his answer was that they needed a greater force of labor to create the portal. They questioned him if that was the only reason, and he answered yes.

This answer did not convince the GCC, so they went to the crucial point of the meeting of that Assembly of why they had decided to activate three atomic bombs to exterminate the Lulus. Anu answered very calmly that they had not activated those bombs to exterminate anyone. They had just had a problem with a Usumgal Anunnaki named Pazuzu who had rebelled against them and tried to steal the Fate Tablets and, not achieving that, he stole three atomic weapons and activated them in revenge.

Anu, also clarified that Pazuzu had been captured and subjected to the death penalty, as the reptilian laws said. Anu finally added that the human race had not been completely exterminated, that there were many survivors, and that, at that time, the repopulation of the Earth was taking place.

It should be noted that the Tablets of Destiny or Me Tablets, were a type of device, a kind of microchip very important in the Anunnaki life since they were the key to activate destructive weaponry, control spacecraft or direct any Anunnaki technological device. In addition, Me Tablets, contained laws and decrees to govern, the most lethal war strategies, weapons instructions, defensive tools to be invulnerable, etc.

These Tablets of Destiny were always used by Anu, Enki, and Enlil; the last one had used them to create terror in humans, subdue them and manipulate them through fear, and so, had forced them to perform human sacrifices.

This microchip, or Me Tablet, was represented in the old engravings as if it were a clock, carrying them on their wrists.

Resuming the Assembly of the Galactic Confederation, the Insectoids questioned Anu about the reason of constructing weapons. Anu gave many explanations, but all without any sense. After a great debate, they came to a conclusion: that the Anunnaki, while repopulating the Earth, should be watched constantly, in addition to that they had to help the Earth to raise its *vibrational level*. Therefore, the Pleiadeans proposed to implant a spy satellite with which they could watch the Anunnaki and emit vibrations to help the Earth.

Although at first the Draconians did not agree with the idea, in the end, they accepted it, on the condition that any member of the Galactic Confederation had access to the information broadcasted by this satellite. The Draconians saw an opportunity with this satellite to keep Anu under surveillance since they did not trust him very much.

The Assembly of that day was closed with this agreement and was convened that within a draconian month there would be another Assembly to decide the fate of the Intraterrestrials and humans.

That it was how they decided that the Moon would be implanted in the Earth, it was taken from a planet located in the Pleiades and transferred to the orbit of the Earth. This mission was entrusted to the Pleiadeans and was started about eleven thousand years ago.

This is why the Atlanteans and Lemurians are known as the Pre-lunar Civilizations.

This agreement to implant the Moon on Earth had a secret goal of the Galactic Confederation against the Reptilians.

While this Assembly was being held, on Earth it had already been three hundred and seventy-one years since Anu had left, since each draconian day equals fifty-three terrestrial years. And in all this time, Marduk started to fall into the temptation offered by humans and the elixir that they emanated when they felt fear, obviously influenced by their uncle, Enlil...

The Backward Evolution of Humankind

While Anu was at that Assembly, Enlil continued with his supreme mandate. He decided to resume mining works focusing on the extraction of gold.

By that time, an Anunnaki explorer had already discovered large gold deposits in what we now know as Africa. During almost four hundred years of absence, of Anu and Enki, the fifth race of human Lulus was used almost completely for works of extraction of gold and in the construction of a road to transport them towards the first Anunnaki settlement located in Iraq.

The more fortunate Lulus were used in this settlement for the construction of large temples where human sacrifices were performed in honor of their reptilian gods.

During Enlil's leadership, knowledge was not transmitted to humans. The only thing that was taught to them was the same belief system that their ancestors had before the Great Flood. This system created by Anu and Enlil was very simple: the humans were created by the Anunnaki gods and they could destroy them if they did not follow their mandates. That is why they had to make human sacrifices to appease their anger.

They were also taught that there were hierarchies within their gods, the supreme god was Anu, then Enki and Enlil, from there, Ninhursag, and so until reaching the minor gods who were the Igigi, the grey ones. In the last step were the hybrids, who were the priests, who had the privilege of not working and were leaders of the humans.

To this belief system, Enlil added the Universal Flood that was taught to the Lulus, as a lesson the gods had given to humans for not obeying their orders.

It should be noted that Enlil prohibited, under pain of death, the pregnancy of Anunnaki females that were caused by human Lulus, since he qualified as an abomination to the children that resulted from this copulation: The Giants.

With this decision, the Giants went extinct of our history. However, what about the Anunnaki males? They could copulate and even impregnate human females. Thing that was not forbidden, but that was not very frequent.

Marduk, on the other hand, finished the seven hundred humans and delivered one hundred and thirty of them to the Intraterrestrials to use them as their slaves. As they had agreed. Also, two Anunnaki geneticists went to the Abzu to teach them the secrets of genetic manipulation. Although obviously, Marduk ordered them to only teach them the basics.

The five hundred and seventy remaining humans were handed over to Enlil and distributed in the first settlement and in different mines of Africa and the Middle East for the mining works.

Marduk developed a close relationship with Enlil, just as his father, Enki, had ordered him. Enlil suspected this sudden approach of his nephew, for which, he started to show him the adorable and irresistible sensation that produced the subtle energies generated by humans when they suffered or were sacrificed.

Marduk, little by little, started to fall into the fascination of human emotions, to the point of almost becoming addicted to it. His favorite sensation was that children emanated just before being sacrificed. In general, it was the sensation most requested by the reptilian Anunnaki.

Marduk realized that Enlil had ordered the creation of numerous temples in honor of him and questioned him why he had done it. He was asked if he wanted to be more revered than his father, Anu. Enlil replied definitely not. They were simply the first of many temples that he would send to build, honoring the main gods. And he informed that the next five temples were to be built in honor of him. Something very convenient for this god addict to human sacrifices.

It should be noted that human sacrifices were made every five or six months, that is, twice a year, however, it was a very short period in relation to the Draconians time that was the time with which the Anunnaki were synchronized.

The gold that was mined was transformed, in its majority, into monoatomic gold, with which the less evolved Anunnaki and older ones could heal, prevent from getting old, and remain more time on the surface of the Earth.

With this Enlil managed to control almost fifty percent of their Anunnaki companions, who were of third, fourth and fifth grade, offering them monoatomic gold in exchange for absolute loyalty. Many Anunnaki reptiles became addicted to this gold. They began to rejuvenate in exchange for losing their psychical abilities, becoming totally controllable.

Marduk was worried because of this since many of his companions were completely zombified (they became addicted to monoatomic gold) and to the service of Enlil. But in reality, Marduk was beginning to feel great envy for Enlil, since he wanted to have as many humans controlled and in service to him as possible. So, he created a plan to take the power of Enlil and Anu and to remain as the only king and god of the Earth.

Meanwhile, the twelve humans who boarded from the Atlantic, in these three hundred and seventy years had already formed several tribes, had discovered the fire and had begun to create basic tools. All this thanks to the previous knowledge that they had from their ancestors, of their ancient civilization; however, not having the technology, they had got stuck. The population was approximately of ten thousand and five hundred people spread over America.

Something similar occurred with the fifteen humans who came to Asia from Mu, they lived much like the Atlanteans who lived in America. They had already discovered the fire, the wheel, basic tools, and weapons to hunt animals. The only difference was the number of inhabitants since in Asia the population reached the twenty-five thousand inhabitants. This is due to the great knowledge that the Lemurians had in medicine and that was transmitted from generation to generation.

Those who practically returned to the Stone Age were the twenty-seven humans who had arrived in Europe, in the boat of Ziusudra, the biblical Noah, since being abandoned by the gods, it took them much effort to start from scratch. The population was about six hundred and fifty people, all nomadic, and dedicated exclusively to hunting.

It should be emphasized that Ziusudra and his direct

descendants were not among them since they were transferred by Enlil to the first Anunnaki settlement shortly after Anu and Enki left. There, they were treated like slaves, but always following the orders of Enlil, and being circumcised generation after generation so that their god could distinguish them from the rest.

When, finally, Anu and Enki returned to the mother ship, about eleven thousand years ago, they were surprised to see many Anunnaki rejuvenated and acting like zombies. Enlil explained to them that it was because of monoatomic gold, with which they could stand longer on the surface of the Earth.

The Anunnaki behaved as if they were at a continuous party. They did not work, many consumed gold, while others were fed with the energy emanating from humans. Everything was happiness for these beings.

Anu, having seen all this, exploded in anger against Enlil screaming that he had disappointed him, since they were in a critical situation and he had organized a great party in his absence. Enlil restrained his anger and only nodded to all the claims of his father.

Anu banned the creation of monoatomic gold and commended to Marduk to supervise the closure of the mining operation. He told everyone to prepare for the arrival of the Pleiadeans. Enki was disappointed to see that Marduk had failed in the assignment he had given to him. And not only that but also noted that Marduk had changed a lot since when he questioned him why he had not tried to stop Enlil in his trait to the Lulus, he answered that humans were simply food for him and that they had no right to possess knowledge. Marduk added: «Father, you have no right to demand that we change the trait to the Lulus since you benefit and nourish yourself with their suffering». Enki answered that he was right that he fed on humans because it was inevitable not to feel pleasure with his emotions detached, but that did not mean that he wanted to have them as mere slaves.

Marduk turned around and came back to Earth to fulfill the task that Anu had given him. Enki realized that Marduk had succumbed to the pleasure humans generated. Also, he realized that he was alone in his pursuit of the evolution of his creation: humans.

Shortly after, the Pleiadeans arrived in the satellite extracted from the Pleiades, that is, on the Moon. And it took fifty-eight Earth years to calibrate it with the same frequency as the Earth and place it in the same cycle of rotation so that only one face was always visible.

Meanwhile, the Carians had arrived on Earth and were surprised that the humans had regressed with respect to their antediluvian predecessors. That is, they did not have the same level of knowledge as their ancestors, so, they decided to talk to Anu, and they told him that before a decision was made about the future of humans, they, the Anunnaki, had the duty to put them at the same level of knowledge they had before causing the explosions. Anu, after a small debate, agreed. He commanded that the Lulus should be trained in basic matters such as Engineering, Astronomy, Agriculture, Construction, etc. so that they could start to evolve.

Enki offered himself to train humans, but Anu firmly opposed. Enki was being watched all the time by two Anunnaki since they arrived on Earth. It is obvious that Anu did not want his children to spoil their plans again.

The Carians went to the Abzu to visit the

Intraterrestrials to explain to them the decision that the Galactic Confederation had taken to implant the Moon on Earth. And, in addition, that they needed their help since they needed to stimulate certain land points to synchronize them with the emissions of the Moon.

The Intraterrestrials were not convinced of this decision, but due to the respect they had for their creators, the Carians, they accepted. Then, the Carians and the Intraterrestrials, from Earth, and the Pleiadeans from the Moonbase, managed to put to work this artificial satellite to try to raise the vibration frequency of the Earth.

The Moon was placed strategically in a position where any point of the Earth could be observed since it not only emitted vibrations but also served as a spy satellite, where they could see everything that happened there.

The Pleiadeans were amazed at the emotional capacity of the humans and their short life, since for them, fifty or eighty Earth years, would be two Pleiadean days. They also lamented the conditions of slavery under which Reptilians had humans, feeding on their lives.

It is obvious that the Pleiadeans were going to vote in favor of the liberation of humankind in the next Assembly.

The Pleiadeans also had a hidden purpose with the implantation of the Moon that was entrusted by the Galactic Confederation and would depend only on the decision made in the next Assembly, the future of humans, to start it or not.

The vibrations of the Moon were captured by the Earth in its great majority through the oceans. That is the reason why the Moon has great influence on ocean tides.

After the implantation of the Moon, the Carians

departed from Earth and prepared for the next Assembly. A group of Pleiadeans remained in control of the Moon's base, while the great majority who had arrived to implant the Moon returned to the Pleiades.

The implantation of the Moon and the constant vigilance of the Pleiadeans delayed Enlil and Marduk's plans to gain control of the Earth.

Fifteen hundred years on Earth passed, which is equivalent to a draconian month, where the Lulus had learned how to build houses, how to harvest land, how to measure time, basic Astronomy, etc. That is, their knowledge and evolutionary conditions had increased. However, they were still being used as slaves and frightened by their reptilian gods, who were offered human sacrifices twice a year, something that the Pleiadeans disliked observing from the Moon.

Meanwhile, Enlil continued to traffic monoatomic gold to his Anunnaki folks, obviously on his father's back, Anu, which helped him continue gaining supporters.

By this time, the Pleiadeans already knew about the existence of the humans who were in America and Asia, however, they decided not to say anything to the Anunnaki, since it seemed that they had not realized that they were there, because they were not submitted.

Just before Anu, Enki, Enlil, and Marduk, together with a caravan of Anunnaki departed to the Assembly of the Galactic Confederation, the Draconians came to the mother ship, who asked Anu for a small demonstration of what humans could give them. Anu gave the order to the Igigi to prepare a great human sacrifice in honor of their guests. The Draconians were satisfied with the taste of human emotions, although disappointed of the size of the

Earth since they considered it too small.

The Draconians told Anu, that Uras, the Earth, would sooner or later become their farm. It did not matter the resolution of the Galactic Confederation. The Earth had to be harvested.

Then, Anu along with his caravan and the Draconians went to the planet Mulge to attend the Assembly where the future of humans would be decided.

That would be the last Assembly held on that planet...

The Extinction of Planet Mulge

The Assembly began with the claims of the Anunnaki Reptilians in the voice of their leader, Anu, who said that the human race lacked sufficient intellect and consciousness to be able to create a civilization that was in harmony with the nature and care of the planet Uras, the Earth. Therefore, they had to be watched by a superior species, and as they had created and accelerated our evolution, they were the best suited to guide us. Otherwise, he warned that humans would destroy the Earth, so they could not let them be a free species.

Suddenly Enki spoke before Anu's astonished eyes and said that it was a lie. That the humans had managed to create two civilizations with free energy and in harmony with the nature of the Earth (obviously remembering the Lemurians and Atlanteans) and said that the Carians could confirm that because they had contemplated these two great civilizations.

Enlil started to shout at Enki accusing him of betrayal, being echoed by the small caravan of Reptilians, including Marduk. The Draconians interrupted the screams and spoke. They asked Enki how the human Lulus had managed to create such a great civilization in such a short time and who had given them that knowledge. To which Enki answered that he had transmitted their knowledge to some of them and others had discovered it by themselves. «That is why they need some guides», the Draconians replied, «

Anu is right. The human Lulus must be guided so that they can evolve, and what better guides than us?»

The Pleiadeans interrupted the Draconians and questioned whether the Anunnaki wanted to be the humans' guides or simply wanted to harvest them to take advantage of them by stealing their subtle energies since they had seen it from the Moon.

The debate turned on at this point and continued for almost two hours, focusing on three main ideas: the first idea was that the Anunnaki Reptilians should be the only guides of humankind to help them evolve, this idea was supported by the Draconians and Insectoids, since these two races had made an arrangement before this Assembly; the second idea was that humans should be guided, but not only by Reptilians, other species could intervene, after all, human Lulus had in their DNA parts of many other extraterrestrial species, this idea was supported by Vegans, Pleiadeans, and Felines; the third main idea was to let the human species free and that they were the owners of their destiny, either to evolve or to become extinct without the help or intervention of another extraterrestrial race, this idea was supported by the Carians and Arcturians.

Enki felt frustrated since part of him wanted humans to be free, but another part wanted to continue with them, guiding them and creating different races. But deep down he knew that none of the three ideas discussed was going to help him or his creation.

By failing to reach a unanimous or majority's agreement of at least five different species, the GCC decided to consult the Kadistu, as the statutes of the Galactic Confederation indicate.

The Draconians were not at all in agreement with this,

since the Kadistu, the life planners, could be very unpredictable, however, the decision they made had to be fulfilled unquestionably. So, they tried to convince the GCC to hold another meeting a later date so that all extraterrestrial species would think about it calmly and, perhaps, a decision would be reached without disturbing the Kadistu. The GCC responded with a resounding NO.

In addition, the GCC asked them about the accusations made by the Pleiadeans and the Carians, about their trait to the Lulus, and that they used them as mere resources for their benefit. Then, the GCC called for a vote to know who was in favor of the Anunnaki leaving the Earth.

The Draconians abruptly interrupted before this vote was done and told the GCC that this was not possible until the Kadistu made a decision, since they did not know if the decision could be that the Anunnaki would be the guides of the humans, something that the Draconians did not know what was going to happen, but they took it as an excuse. So they were not going to retire from Uras until the Kadistu gave their verdict.

The Galactic Confederation accepted since they did not really believe that the Kadistu would make the decision that the Anunnaki should be the guides of the humans. Then it was only a matter of time that they left the Earth. And he told the Anunnaki that they had to fix their mistake, since the Lulus had lost thousands of terrestrial years of evolution, and that, in human parameters, was a lot of time. So they ordered to transmit the necessary knowledge so that humans could create a civilization, and they could corroborate if what Enki said was true.

Anu replied that he had already passed on much

knowledge to humans, but they were not capable of creating a civilization. The Galactic Confederation then decided to call for a vote to know who was in favor of transmitting only the necessary knowledge to the Lulus to begin their evolution.

Five species agreed on that, and the GCC gave Enki this task. And entrusted the Pleiadeans the supervision from the Moon.

Enki was happy, he was finally able to help his creation. The Reptilians and Draconians had lost a battle, but not the war. Before the Assembly was over, the Pleiadeans alerted the Galactic Confederation of a large asteroid that had been discovered near Jupiter's orbit and was traveling at great speed to the planet Mulge, and that, according to their calculations, there was a ninety percent probability of impact with this planet in approximately thirty Earth months. So the Confederation entrusted the Pleiadeans the destruction of this asteroid once it crossed Jupiter's orbit.

Mulge was an inhospitable planet, located between Mars and Jupiter, in which, the Galactic Confederation installed a base to exploit their resources. And they wanted to create a gigantic headquarters, which would guard all the problems that arose in the Milky Way. That is why the assemblies were held on this big planet.

When the decision to create this headquarters was made, the Draconians did not agree so upon hearing the news about that asteroid going to Mulge, they decided to take revenge.

The Assembly finished and the Anunnaki returned to Earth accompanied by a group of Carians. Before they left, the Draconians told Anu to obey all the orders of the

Carians until they knew the resolution of the Kadistu.

The Draconians, later, met in Orion with the Insectoids, and there they planned how to prevent the Pleiadeans from destroying the asteroid that had 15.700 kilometers of radius —much larger than the planet Earth— so that it would impact the planet Mulge, which had about sixty-five thousand kilometers of radius. Undoubtedly, this would lead to the destruction of this planet.

And so it was. The Draconians ordered the Insectoids to put artifacts on the asteroid, which, when activated would create an electromagnetic field around it so that the radars and digital telescopes of the Galactic Confederation and the Pleiadeans would not detect it.

Once this was done, the Draconians waited for the Pleiadeans to destroy this asteroid. Twenty-four terrestrial months had passed after the Assembly in Mulge when three Pleiadean ships loaded with nuclear weapons left their bases in the Pleiades and headed towards the asteroid to destroy it. Once they approached the asteroid, they were ambushed by five draconian ships which destroyed the Pleiadean ships in a few minutes. And just after having destroyed them, they activated the artifacts to create the electromagnetic field around the asteroid and hide it from the radars and digital telescopes of the Pleiadeans and the Galactic Confederation, which, at that moment was in Sirius.

All of them celebrated the destruction of this asteroid, the Pleiadeans informed the Confederation that the operation had been a success. Although they had lost communication with the three ships that destroyed the asteroid. So they told them they would send a scout ship to go to the place to investigate.

The Galactic Confederation also told the Pleiadeans that they had lost communication with Mulge and that this was surely due to the great explosion caused by nuclear weapons.

At the same time that the Draconians destroyed the Pleiadean ships, the Insectoids disabled all communications of the planet Mulge.

Cheating had been a success. The Draconians plan worked out to perfection. The scout ship that had been sent to investigate the three ships that were sent to destroy the asteroid, was also ambushed and destroyed by the Draconians.

When the Pleiadeans lost communication with the scout ship, they began to suspect that something was wrong. So, they decided to give notice to the Galactic Confederation. And when they realized that the asteroid had not been destroyed it was too late. The asteroid impacted the planet Mulge approximately 9.500 years ago, causing it to start fragmenting into pieces and these were launched to space. One of these pieces impacted on Mulge's moon, it completely removed it from its natural orbit and placed it in a new orbit, right between Mercury and the Earth.

This Moon became then as what we know today as the planet Venus. And the millions of pieces that remained of the planet Mulge became what we know today as the Asteroid Belt.

In this way, the dream of the Galactic Confederation to build a base in the Milky Way had ended. The Carians, the Pleiadeans, and the Arcturians suspected that the sabotage to destroy the great asteroid had been the work of the Draconians, though they did not have enough evidence to accuse them.

Almost eighteen hundred Earth years were left before the next meeting of the Grand Council of the Galactic Confederation with the Kadistu where the destiny of humankind would be completely defined...

The Final Decision of the Kadistu

After finishing the Assembly of the Galactic Confederation, a group of Carians came to Earth with the Anunnaki commanded by Anu.

The task of the Carians was to transmit their knowledge so that the Lulu humans began to evolve, as they had agreed at the Assembly. However, shortly after the Carians began with this arduous task, they found out that Mulge had been destroyed by the asteroid that the Pleiadeans were to disintegrate, so they began to suspect that something was not right. They decided to return to their planet located in Orion to investigate what was happening, leaving in Uras, the Earth, just four emissaries to transmit their knowledge to humans.

Before the return of the Carians to their planet, Anu saw the perfect opportunity to completely stop the plan to teach humans to look after themselves alone, for which, he entrusted Enlil to tell all the Anunnaki not to help in this task, but in a discreet way. Enlil gave notice to all his followers to do so.

During the time of waiting for the interview with the Kadistu, on Earth, Enlil and Marduk were frustrated and desperately worried about their plans not being carried out. The two had to wait for the Kadistu's verdict.

Something similar happened to Enki because he felt that his creation was being wasted and he could not help it since he was constantly being watched by the Anunnaki who were faithful to Anu.

On one occasion, he managed to get away from his watchers and take advantage of it to see how much the Atlanteans that were in America and the Lemurians who were in Asia had evolved, and he was surprised to see that, while the Atlanteans in America had evolved very little in all this time, their population was increasing; however, the Lemurians who had developed in technology, hunting and gathering had their population on a decline. So he decided to investigate it and discovered that the Lemurians were dying because of a rare disease and that it was spreading rapidly among all of them. Due to the short time he had, he could not investigate more of this disease and how it had originated. He began to take DNA samples from Lemurians, healthy and sick and asked for support from Intraterrestrials since his laboratory was closed by Anu's orders. In addition, he was forbidden to experiment with humans since the creation of the fifth race. For this reason, he asked for help from the Intraterrestrials, because he knew that they were the only ones who were carrying out genetic experiments on the Abzu.

When he arrived with them, he was surprised to see that they had already created in the laboratory several species of animals and when asked what they were going to do with them, they answered that they were going to be released on the surface of the Earth. That is, they were increasing the diversity of life on Earth.

Enki asked the Intraterrestrials to help him detect the rare disease that was killing the Lemurians. The Intraterrestrials refused because they did not know anything about human physiology, and what they had studied about it was very little.

After a long negotiation, the Intraterrestrials accepted the samples from the Lemurians and told Enki that they were going to do everything they could. Enki gave them the samples and went back to his mother ship since he had been absent longer than he could.

Seventy Earth years later, Enki escaped again and went to the Abzu to see the advances of the Intraterrestrials. There they showed Enki a new human race, created with Lemurian DNA and human DNA that the Intraterrestrials had in the Abzu. They explained that this new breed had been improved in their immune system and that they were immune to the disease that was killing them.

Enki at first was upset because by mixing these two types of DNA, this new hybrid race had lost the codons that it had activated, leaving in it only twenty. This caused them to decrease their stature considerably. Enki, annoyed, told them that he had asked them to investigate the disease, not to create a new race, to which they responded that they were not experts in human physiology and that had been their solution. However, if he wanted, they could destroy the ten humans they had created genetically.

Enki seeing that he had no other option, calmed down and kindly requested them to create forty men and forty more women and put them on the surface of the Earth. It was born, then, the sixth and last race of humans, with a yellow complexion, slanted eyes, and an improved immunological system. Enki released the eighty humans in Asia, next to the Lemurians, it should be mentioned, and they had already lost sixty percent of their population.

Therefore, the population remained distributed on

Earth as follows: seventy percent was in the first settlement, located in what we know today as Iraq; eight percent were made up of slaves who were left in the African zone and who did not return to the first settlement; twelve percent were the Atlanteans that were in America; five percent were the Lemurians who were in Asia; and the remaining five percent were the humans who arrived on Ziusudra's boat and who were not returned to the first settlement because they were not the Chosen People.

During almost two thousand terrestrial years of waiting for the decision of the Kadistu, the humans did not manage to evolve in almost anything. The Carians basically taught them to teach them advanced mathematics, but due to the constant obstacles that the Anunnaki put, this was very complicated. Humans were not even near creating a civilization on their own.

The date arrived. Eighteen hundred Earth years had passed after the last Assembly of the Galactic Confederation and the leaders of the Great GCC were ready to speak with the Kadistu. This meeting was held in the Pleiades, one of the great venues of the Galactic Confederation.

The Great GCC communicated with the Kadistu through an extra artifact made of crystal, since the Kadistu were in the fifth dimension. And it is very unpleasant for them to endure the enormous density that exists in the third and fourth dimension, for which they prefer to communicate through this device.

These meetings with the Kadistu were held once each Pleiadean year, which is equivalent to one draconian year and a half, which is the same to twenty-nine thousand and forty-four terrestrial years. And there were discussed all the problems that existed in the galaxy. And for which, the GCC needed a guide or help to solve them.

In this last meeting, among many other topics, came out the destiny of humankind. The GCC explained to the Kadistu that humans were a new conscious species in the universe and that they had not agreed on whether to guide them or let them forge their destiny, so they needed their help to make the decision.

The Kadistu answered that being humans a conscious species, they had the right to make their own decisions and to forge their own destiny, whether it was evolving or becoming extinct. And if it was a race that was worth keeping, they had to prove it.

So they dictated a law: that all extraterrestrial races should respect the free will of humans; and made it clear that if humans wanted to be guided by other superior races, so it was going to be. And if they did not want it, they should also respect it.

They also made clear that the higher extraterrestrial races could only intervene if humans put the life of planet Earth at risk. Otherwise, they had to respect the free will of humankind.

That is how the fate of humans was sentenced to free will 7.700 years ago. Something that the Draconians celebrated greatly since they were skilled manipulators and knew that human Lulus were manageable.

The Pleiadeans and Carians were not very satisfied with this resolution of the Kadistu since they considered that humankind was not sufficiently conscious and had been manipulated since its creation to let them take their destiny into their hands. However, they had to abide by this decision.

The Draconians informed the Anunnaki of the decision made by the Kadistu and began to give precise orders to Anu to start forming the human farm they wanted.

The Carians, for their part, decided to take advantage of this resolution of the Kadistu and decided to send a group of 150 Carians to begin transmitting the basic knowledge to humankind so that they could begin their evolution. Something that the Anunnaki could no longer avoid since humans were the ones who had to decide if they wanted to be taught or not.

The Arcturians who were aware of the whole human problem, Lulus, but who had nevertheless remained aloof, decided to take advantage of the Kadistu's sentence to send a caravan of twenty emissaries to planet Earth and so on to be able to study humans better. This caravan was amazed to see the potential that humans had and the ability to feel and express feelings. A great number of these Arcturians emissaries succumbed to the pleasures that humans gave to detach the subtle energies and the taste of their blood, which, basically, focused on humans who were practically abandoned in Africa and they were dedicated to guiding them in exchange for them feeding them.

Their favorite dish always were the children, from which they sucked all the blood of the body.

The Pleiadeans, on the other hand, had a secret plan to drive the Anunnaki out of the Earth but decided not to carry it out until seeing how things went on Earth to determine if they were going to put it to action or not.

Enki, upon learning of the resolution of the Kadistu,

decided to help the Carians to pass on their knowledge to the humans who were in the first settlement since his idea was to let the Atlanteans and Lemurians free to see how they evolved by themselves. Something that did not last for a long time.

Anu could not prevent Enki from helping the Carians since he had to respect the free will of humankind. However, he sent two of his emissaries to have Enki under surveillance at all times and inform him of all his movements.

So, after two thousand years after the resolution of the Kadistu, humankind had made the greatest evolutionary leap in its history. The Sumerian civilization had been born.

Despite the great technological advances and knowledge that humans had achieved, they still lived fearful of their gods and they continued to offer sacrifices.

While this civilization was born, Enlil and Marduk, each for their part, were waiting for the right moment to take control of the Earth…

The Expulsion of the Anunnaki from Uras, Earth

Despite being Sumerians the first civilization in human history —approximately five thousand years ago— and despite their great evolutionary leap, these were still being dominated by the Anunnaki, through their vassal hybrids.

These hybrids were on the cusp of its social system, were the Supreme rulers and considered demigods for having Anunnaki blood.

They were also afraid of them since they considered them people with superhuman and immortal powers.

Religion helped a lot to have the Sumerians under control, as it inculcated them a fear rooted in all their gods, and therefore, they should give them sacrifices each certain time.

Anu ordered to write Anunnaki history and how we had been created to root more religion among the Sumerians to make them, the Anunnaki, be supreme gods, and so their story would be preserved for posterity. So they began to write the Sumerian clay tablets.

Many of the texts were narrated to human scribes by Anu himself. And many other texts were narrated by various Anunnaki gods as Inanna, Enlil, Ninhursag, etc.

It is worth mentioning, that most of the stories written in the Sumerian tablets were deliberately exaggerated by these gods, to denote their power.

The Sumerians used highly advanced technology, inherited by the gods with which could create great temples and buildings as the Ziggurat. However, they did not understand how the technology worked, that is, they knew how to use it but they did not understand its functioning.

So, together Enki and the Carians began to teach the Sumerians science, as advanced mathematics, physics, chemistry, etc... They started to teach them the basics so they could understand how these extraterrestrial technologies worked.

The Pleiadeans reported Arcturian leaders about the behavior their emissaries were having on Earth. Therefore, they ordered them to immediately leave the Earth and leave humans alone, and they did so, but not before inheriting their knowledge, customs, language, and beliefs to the human Lulus who were in Africa.

Little had changed things with the resolution of the Kadistu. It is true that the humans were now living in a social system and had some more advanced knowledge. However, they continued to be dominated and manipulated by the Anunnaki.

Until one day, nearly a hundred fifty years after the creation of Sumer, at an event where one of the high priests, a hybrid ruler of Sumer, was walking among the slaves, one of them named Isaki managed to get in front of the high priest and without any scruple, he took a spear and threw it right in the chest of the ruler causing him to die. Next moment, this slave started to scream that the gods and demigods were not immortal, honoring the crowd and causing a large revolt.

A part of Sumerian slaves had awakened, and they realized that their rulers, who everybody feared were just like them, and died just like them. The news quickly spread over Sumer, causing great unrest throughout the city putting at risk the pyramidal system imposed by their gods.

The Anunnaki for the first time in their history had fear of going down to Earth since they were afraid that the humans could attack them. Anu was furious and blamed the Carians for having planned the murder. He knew perfectly that he could not attack humans due to the resolution of the Kadistu, and that there were many alien races watching, so he created a plan to fix it.

The Carians and Pleiadeans from the Moonbase celebrated this event since humans had taken the first step towards their liberation.

Enki was surprised about this event and had mixed feelings, since on the one hand he looked forward to his creation putting resistance to be enslaved, and on the other hand he felt worried because he knew perfectly that the human Lulus, by using violence, could become a very dark breed in the future if they wanted to.

Anu ordered Enlil to take some hybrids and slaves from Sumer who were worshipers of the gods and settle them in another place to start everything again.

Enlil saw a magnificent opportunity to implement his plan. So not only the hybrids, but he also moved his *chosen people*, who were faithful to him and brought them to settlements located on the banks of the Middle River and bass of the Nile River. And he started to lead hybrids to begin the construction of a new civilization. In order to achieve this, they could use as slaves his *chosen people*. Egypt was born.

Marduk, took this opportunity to convince Anu to let him take several people from Sumer and create a new city far from the chaos that this civilization had become and to continue benefiting from humans, to which Anu agreed.

Marduk persuaded a handful of men and women and took them to a location near to Sumer, where he established the city of Akkad.

In Sumer, forty percent of the population had ceased to believe in the gods and began to work for their own account, and another sixty percent, fearful of the wrath of the gods was still faithful to the imposed pyramidal system.

Unfortunately for Anu, the Draconians went to his mother ship to see how things were going in Uras, and quickly, the Draconians named humans as the *Sag - Giga*, which means *the village of blackheads* because from the mother ship human heads were black because of the hair. Besides that, they realized that the sacrifices had gone down considerably and that the humans had advanced considerably with respect to their last visit. Because of that Anu was told to divide the humans so they ordered him to begin with their communication system; if they could not understand themselves, they could never be together.

Anu got perfectly the idea. However, he had a problem, since the Anunnaki had only two dialects from the Emešà, their mother tongue dialects; these were the Emenite and the Emesal. So he ordered Enlil to teach the Emenite to the new civilization that was growing near the Nile River. And he told Ninhursag to help Marduk to teach the Emesal to residents of the new city of Akkad.

Enki suspected that Marduk was plotting something, so he ordered the ruler of Sumer to build a wall around the city, anticipating what was going to happen.

The Draconians volunteered to help transmit one of their languages to the sag-giga humans, so they focused on the inhabitants who were in Asia, who had not been manipulated nor been indoctrinated, yet had evolved considerably. It was the perfect opportunity to start manipulating them.

Fortunately, the Draconians did not have enough patience to train these humans. So, they limited to convey the language and teach them to make sacrifices, obviously. Enki did not agree on having different languages between humans, so he claimed that to Anu, and he replied that he was only teaching them new ways of communicating and that he was not forcing them to anything. It depended on them whether they accepted it or not.

Enki knew perfectly that he could not stop this, so he devoted himself to travel in his ship from one place to another to teach and pass on his knowledge to humans of all over the world, starting with the humans who were in Europe and which were less advanced technologically. Humankind began to call him *Hermes Trismegistus, the thrice-time* great because of all the knowledge he taught.

Only one hundred years after the arrival of humans to the banks of the Nile, a new civilization was born and its name was Egypt. The quick creation of this civilization was mostly due to the extraterrestrial technology that Enlil had provided them because he wanted to build three pyramids perfectly aligned to the Orion constellation so everybody would remember where their gods came from.

For this purpose, Enlil taught the Egyptians a new system of belief, very similar to the Sumerian one but with different gods. Although in reality they were the same only with different names. For example, Anu was Ra; Osiris,

Set, and Anubis were Enlil; Horus and Thoth were Enki; etc. But obviously maintaining the main objective of having people frightened so that they offered them sacrifices.

This, Enlil had already planned it with Anu since the Draconians wanted humans to have different belief systems so that they could never unify.

The social system was pyramidal, very similar to the Sumerian in which at the top were the Pharaohs. But the only difference was that this Egyptian system was more slaver, as the chosen people of Enlil had to work more than 12 hours a day for a minimum payment of wheat.

The Carians, worried about Enki being so involved in the construction of Egypt, spent a lot of time visiting this civilization and trying to awake the population. Because of that, the Egyptians also identified them as gods. Even Horus was drawn and described as a Carian.

While all of this was happening in Egypt, Marduk had already led to the Akkadians to build a great city, almost as important as Uruk in Sumer. He had taught them the same system of beliefs the Sumerians had with the only difference that the main god was not Anu, but for them it was Marduk.

Anu realized that this city was growing very fast and they revered more Marduk than him, so he summoned him to question him that, to which Marduk replied that it was a decision that the Akkadians had taken and that he had nothing to do. Anu did not believe him. But he could only threaten him and tell him not to dare to challenge his power.

All the Anunnaki were amazed by the Majesty of Egyptian civilization. Marduk took advantage of that to convince the Akkadians that began to create weapons secretly. The plan to be the one God was going on. Marduk had already achieved great power thanks to the subtle energies that all the Akkadians gave to him. He even had won followers among the Anunnaki, more because of fear of him than out of respect, so he was convinced of taking Anu out from power.

On the year two thousand three hundred and fifty-three BC, Marduk convinced a man called Zargon to attack Uruk and all the Sumer cities. So, he did it. He took the weapons that the Akkadians had created and with a numerous army started the war, leaving a great slaughter and suffering behind. Zargon beat all the Sumerian cities with the exception of Uruk which was already surrounded by a great wall and that made her almost impervious to the attacks of the Akkadians.

The Draconians and the Anunnaki were marveled by the huge negative subtle energies that the suffering and death of humans gave off. So much time had passed since the last time there was a large amount of energy for them. That last time was when the tree nuclear weapons exploded, causing the great flood.

Anu and Enlil, meanwhile, were furious, since they knew that Marduk was behind all of this even though he denied it outright. However, seeing that his Akkadian army could not trespass Uruk's great wall, he desperately offered him one of the Me Tablets he had stolen, only in that way they could take over all Sumer.

The Akkadian empire, the first empire in the world had been born.

Anu, upon finding out that Marduk had stolen a Destiny's Tablet, condemned him to prison. Marduk's plan was that his allies stole the Destiny's Tablets that were left and, in that way, taking over the mothership. But Enlil anticipated this and managed to capture all the Anunnaki allies of Marduk and prevented this to happen. Marduk was captured and taken before Anu, who had sentenced him to death. However, the Draconians interceded for him, saying that Marduk had taught them something, that humans could feed them without sacrifices. They just had to be convinced of fighting each other so they could be benefited.

Anu was furious for Marduk's disobedience, but as the Draconians were on his side, he sentenced him to exile, for which Marduk was grateful because being alive, he could regain strength with all the sacrifices the great Akkadian empire offered to him and come back to overthrow Anu.

Marduk was exiled from the Earth and the mothership, but not before having *taught them* beings the benefits of war.

The Pleiadeans, having seen the killing and suffering the humans had done, could not tolerate it anymore, since they knew they were being manipulated by the Anunnaki. So, they decided to put on work the plan to expel definitely the Anunnaki and Draconians from Earth. They and the Intraterrestrials activated hundreds of antennas they had installed in the Abzu and started to produce low-frequency electromagnetic waves from the Moon to the Earth with the sole purpose that this would make it vibrate at an increasingly dense frequency, so high, that for the Anunnaki and any extraterrestrial race would be impossible to tolerate.

The Anunnaki realized that, as the time passed by, it

was more difficult to be on Earth. They knew that their vibration was changing. The first to realize was Enki, so he decided to do several things before leaving Earth. One of them was visiting the Atlanteans in America and giving them the technology to build great stone buildings. The second thing was creating a secret society in Egypt at which he would not only teach science to humans but also the secrets of the universe, the spirit, death, and matter. *The Brotherhood of the White Dragon* was born.

And the last thing he did was discover the Chosen People of Enlil since he had discovered that his brother had a group of very loyal humans and that at some point he was going to use them one way or another. So, he tried to recruit some of these humans at the back of Enlil, which was very hard. However, he managed to recruit several of them and led them to the western shore of the Dead Sea, where he founded a town known as the Essenes.

The Draconians were furious because of the vibration change of the Earth. They knew that sooner or later they would have to abandon it. Due to that, he taught Anu and Enlil rituals so that humans could communicate with them, only that there was a problem, these rituals would only work if the communication was between different dimensional levels and only on specific days along the year.

Enlil taught passed on and taught these rituals to members of his people and the great priests of Egypt, and told them to communicate with him on those exact days.

Anu was worried about what the reaction of the Draconians would be since they were one step away from losing their human farm. In just 60 years the vibration of the Earth was so dense that the Anunnaki had to leave the Earth. They even had to take their mothership out of the orbit of the Earth.

The humans were free at last. Or at least that is what the Pleiadeans thought.

The Draconians, furious, knew that the Pleiadeans were responsible for that. So they made a complaint to the Galactic Confederation saying that the Pleiadeans had violated the Human Free Will law. The Galactic Confederation promised to analyze the claim and make a decision.

Enki was tired of everybody making decisions to change the destiny of his creation. So he finally decided to liberate once and forever the humankind. He knew that although he could not be close to the Earth, he could communicate with the humans through *the phase*. That is how he started his most ambitious plan to liberate humankind, a plan that would change the history of the world forever...

The Birth of the Messiah

Expelled from the Earth, the Anunnaki and the Draconians as result of the Pleiadeans' plan and the support of the Intraterrestrials, the Anunnaki were stationed about 560,000 kilometers from the Earth. And from there, Enki tried to communicate through the phase with some humans on Earth but he had no success because the enormous distance between them could not connect them using the *astral projection* to make contact through dreams, as it had done many times before from his mothership.

At this distance the subtle energies that the humans gave off could not be captured or perceived by the Anunnaki nor the Draconians, that's why Enlil came up to the idea of creating a suit that could eliminate the negative effect that the vibrations of moon produced on them. Something that the Draconians did not approve since they had another plan. Anu was told he would be transferred along with the rest of the Anunnaki caravan to the astral bottom of the fourth dimension to escape the electromagnetic waves emitted by the Moon, and from there they would capture the subtle energies of the human and deliver them to them.

Anu told them that was not possible because their bodies were not so evolved to move between dimensions. The Draconians informed him that they already had the technology to travel to the fourth dimension without having an interdimensional body. Anu, amazed, realized of all the time that had passed in Uras, the Earth, he had forgotten the technological advances that the Draconians could have reached as well, so he was unable to do other than to imagine it.

Enlil asked them why they had to be in the astral bottom. The Draconians explained to him that, as the dimensions are interconnected, the lower is the frequency, the closer will be the lower dimension. That is, the astral bottom of the fourth dimension is the closest to the third dimension. Being in the astral center of the fourth dimension, they would be further and at the risk of not being able to capture the energies of the humans. And, while in the astral top of the fourth dimension it would be closer to the fifth dimension than the third and possibly their bodies would not resist it. In addition, they said that the rituals they taught humans to communicate with them only worked when performed between two adjacent dimensions.

Their plan was simple: once installed in the fourth dimension, the Anunnaki could see everything humans did, however, they would be invisible to human eyes, since being in a higher dimension, and these would be imperceptible to the lower dimensions. However, they could materialize in the third dimension through the rituals that humans made on specific dates.

Enlil asked what would happen if educated humans did not perform those rituals. The Draconians answered them that if that happened, they would have lost to the human farm.

In other words, they were going to take the risk of going to the fourth dimension to depend on the free will of the human Lulus.

Such an irony...

The Draconians led Anu, Enlil, and Enki alongside other thirteen Anunnaki to Orion into a machine that would take them to the fifth dimension. And the Anunnaki who refused to leave were left on a moon of Jupiter, now known under the name of Europe, where they were used as slaves in the huge bases that the Draconians had in that satellite.

The plan went on, and the reptile Anunnaki were transferred from Orion to the fourth dimension. It took the Anunnaki almost five hundred Earth years to adapt their body to this new dimension. Once done, Enki began to try to connect with the dreams of humans to communicate with them. It took him some time, but he was successful. He managed to connect through the phase with two humans: one man located on the European continent, paradoxically, the less developed of the continents at that time; and also communicated with one of the Essenes disciples.

Enki knew that not being present among humans and only being able to communicate with a few who had *the gift*, knowledge would have to be passed from man to man, and from generation to generation. So he first passed a lot of knowledge on the first man in Europe and, later, asked him to form a group of ten more men to whom he should convey all the knowledge acquired. And finally ordered that each of those men began to instruct and teach others, the younger the best. Thus the first schools were born, the first masters and first apprentices.

This method was so effective and the knowledge delivered by Enki was so vast, that just over six hundred years, this group of wise humans, had already created the great Greek civilization, where one of the pillars was the transmission of knowledge, the Government was focused on the decisions of the people, and it was the first civilization that did not have slaves. Parallel to this, during this time, he was transmitting knowledge to the Essenes that managed to communicate with him, focused on increasing their psychic and spiritual power.

Generation after generation, he tried to share their knowledge so that they could evolve, since his plan was that some of them could become Christified. That is, reach Nirvana and show the way to all humankind for their liberation and evolution.

While the Essenes had managed a psychical and spiritual breakthrough as the power to heal with their hands, telekinesis, etc. they had not been able to even touch the Christification line. Enki became aware that the problem was in the codons of the DNA that humans had connected, that did not allow them to activate their pineal gland. This plan of Enki was very ambitious, as if achieved, human beings could come to overtake the Anunnaki.

While this was happening with Enki, Anu and the other Anunnaki, managed to communicate with the humans who performed the rituals twice a year: once in the Equinox and another on the Solstice. In fact, those who performed these rituals were mostly hybrids that had been trained by and were faithful to the Anunnaki and they were basically ordered to introduce human sacrifices in Asia, which followed the massacres to the Akkadians, oppression in Egypt, etc.

The Anunnaki continued manipulating humankind to be always in conflict and thus, they could capture the subtle negative energies of the human. These negative energies were trapped by the Anunnaki in the fourth dimension with some containers that the Draconians gave them. Once filled, they were carried by Enki to Orion and delivered to the Draconians. Although on many occasions the Draconians themselves arrived in the fourth dimension to pick up these containers.

Negative energy collected from humans was much smaller than the one that existed when the Anunnaki were on Earth. And this bothered to the Draconians since their farm did not give the benefits that they expected. So they told Anu to introduce the concept of money and told him that all human transactions had to be replaced with metal balls. Then Anu ordered the hybrids in one of their rituals to introduce the concept of money and the currency around the world.

The first to use this concept were the Asian civilizations in the 700 B.C, approximately. And it quickly began to be used in Egypt, Acadia and neighboring towns.

The Draconians knew that through this simple concept of money they could raise on humans their darkest and most twisted side and that it would help to have them more controlled. And so they would be easier to manipulate for squeezing them all their negative energy. And so was born the most powerful control over humankind, money method.

At that time, Egypt kept growing, by pressing their slaves, and strictly following their polytheist religion. Although human sacrifices and animals were drastically reduced.

The Akkadians were expanding their empire, fighting all the tribes and towns they found, although their rivals were less and less. This greatly reduced the negative energy emanated by humankind. Also, they continued worshiping Marduk as their major god. However, this changed and other gods like Anu and Enlil began to be worshipped more and more.

Asians had already created several different civilizations. And they were led by dynasties. Always in conflict with each other. The art of war was always a constant among Asians. In addition to more sacrifices, most of them, performed with animals.

The Americans had already created three large settlements: one located in Peru, one in Central America, and other in North America. Despite having the technology to create large buildings of stone, there had been little progress. Over time, they had lost much of the knowledge inherited by Enki.

The Americans had already advanced, but still had not managed to create a civilization. And finally, the Europeans, who were further behind humans at that time, with the knowledge delivered by Enki gave a great evolutionary leap. They had already created the most humanist civilizations in history, the Greek civilization.

Enlil intuited that Enki had something to do with the evolution of this civilization. So he began to follow him more closely. Towards 1.200 B.C, Enlil discovered how Enki communicated with humans throughout the phase. This was a unique opportunity for his interests, so he decided not to tell anything to Anu, and decided to learn how to communicate across the phase. After much practice, Enlil was able to control the phase and tried repeatedly to communicate with a member of his chosen people. All without success. His first contact was established with a man who was the brother of the future

Pharaoh of Egypt. His name was Moses. And it was so much the manipulation introduced by Enlil that he managed to convince him that he was, in fact, a Hebrew and that his mission was to release his chosen people. He took him from Egypt and sent him to Syria where once it had been the first Anunnaki settlement. Just for him to get one of the tools that were used to create an electromagnetic field and levitate stones. And, with that, create large buildings.

However, Enlil had actually been able to deceive Moses saying that it was a very powerful weapon that would protect him from his enemies. This trip took Moses quite a while, and at his return to Egypt, his brother was already the Pharaoh. Strictly following the instructions of Enlil, he threatened his brother Ramses telling him to release the Hebrews —that was how the people faithful to Enlil called themselves— otherwise, he would suffer the wrath of their god. Ramses obviously ignored the warning of his brother, so Moses poured into the waters of the Nile River a chemical that had been prepared with his own hands following the instructions of Enlil. This substance caused all the fish in the river to die instantly, dying red the water because of the blood of these dead fish. In addition, many amphibians such as frogs came out of the river and began to invade the Egyptians crops.

A large number of dead fish attracted a large number of flies and insects to Egypt, causing a real plague. This, coupled with a huge hail storm that coincidentally occurred in the afternoon, caused that many people close to the Pharaoh who had heard the threat of Moses attributed all these phenomena to the wrath of his god.

Moses who was already known by almost all Jews, met

Ramses again, and once more asked him to release his people otherwise his god's wrath would fall more forcefully about Egypt.

Ramses refused outright. So, instructed by Enlil, Moses asked all the Hebrews that night to sacrifice a lamb and with its blood to put a visible mark on the doors of their homes, since only those who had that mark would be saved from the wrath of his god.

Once the night came, a group chosen by Moses began to fireballs of paper wrapped inside the same chemical that he poured into the Nile River and they started to throw them to all the houses that didn't have the mark of blood, including the house of the pharaoh, since the guards did not oppose to Moses and allowed him to enter out of fear of his god.

This caused the death of many people. Most of them were children who could not resist the toxic gases of this chemical. The rumors and the fear quickly spread all over Egypt. And those events were attributed to the god of the Hebrews. Ramses, awash in fear, seeing his son on the edge of death decided to free the Hebrews and let them go. His plan was to corner them along the Red Sea and mow them down there, out of the sight of the Egyptian.

The exodus of the chosen people begun. And arriving at the Red Sea, they were ambushed by the Egyptian cavalry. Then Moses used the weapon his God gave him and realized that while he approached the sea, this created a field that divided it in two and allowed a passage through it. So they went to the narrowest part of the sea and crossed it running.

Most of Egyptian who saw this miracle stopped. However, a few dared to continue the persecution. And once Moses deactivated this artifact, the Red Sea went again together, burying his pursuers.

Once they crossed the Red Sea, Moses led them to Mount Sinai, as his god had commanded. And he climbed it to receive new orders. It took him forty days to carve on a stone the commandments dictated to him by his god. There, for the first time, Moses asked Enlil his name, and he replied to Yahweh, which means *"I am"*. And he said to Moses that those commandments had to be literally accepted, solely by his chosen people.

These miracles caused such an impact in the world of that time that the word spread quickly. The god of the Hebrews was the only one and he had given those Commandments for all humankind. These commandments were thought by Enlil to have completely controlled all his people. Later, Enlil, Yahweh, told Moses to lead his people to the desert where he had them walk for forty years to test their faith. Something that he loved doing to Enlil. He finally led them to Canaan and it was there where the twelve tribes of Israel established and the Jewish were born.

The subtle energies increased greatly with all these events and Anu suspected that the liberation of these slaves was the work of Enki, although later he realized that it was not so. An excellent plot of Enlil.

Enki was completely bewildered. So he began to investigate that so-called god Yahweh that had caused all this. Anu, worried about the great evolution of the Greek civilization started to see them as a great threat to the interests of the Anunnaki. He then ordered Enlil to corrupt it.

Enlil began to infiltrate several hybrids and members

of his *chosen people* so that they could to indoctrinate the Greeks through religion and worship of the gods. And so it began the Greek mythology. But Enlil was not satisfied with that. He wanted to break them from the inside, breaking their spirit. And this was achieved by promoting debauchery and purely physical practices as homosexuality or pederasty.

Little by little the Greek people became corrupt and separated from his spiritual teachings and originally humanist.

After five hundred years of the emergence of the Greek civilization, this was not remotely similar to what it was in its beginning. Since they were totally indoctrinated worshiping false gods and creating weapons to have an army and thus conquer their enemies.

Enki seeing this, instructed a group of Greek sages to steer towards the South. Specifically in Rome, so they could create another civilization with the same principles of ancient Greece.

And so on the year 500 B.C, approximately, it was established the Roman Republic, which for 450 years followed the precepts of Justice and humankind that had received from Enki. However, he knew that it was a matter of time for the Anunnaki to manipulate and corrupt this new civilization.

Enki realized that the only hope was to show the Christification to humans. So he decided to play his last card. In one of the trips to Orion to deliver the containers to the Draconians, Enki asked for help from the Carians. Since he wanted to create another human with the characteristics of the first race, which had thirty-two DNA codons active. Enki had calculated that for his plan to be effective, he would have to create another human with at least thirty active codons.

Many Carians refused since they believed that it was against the rules of the Kadistu. Enki explained to them that this human would be born only if humans wanted so. A small group of Carians decided to help and support the plan of Enki.

After several trips to Orion delivering containers, Enki received the news that the Carians finally had the genetic material, which, according to their calculations, could create a very similar human to the original race. Enki took the DNA sample and asked for help from the Pleiadeans, and it was that how the Anunnaki continued manipulating humankind, but now from the fourth dimension.

During this time the Pleiadeans had lost hope in humankind for all they had done in the Earth, but upon finding out about the Anunnaki manipulation, many of them decided to help Enki.

During all the time this plan had been carried out, the Anunnaki already had complete control of the Roman Republic and had turned it into a great empire. Conquering Greece by the year 146 B. C, and conquering the Egyptian civilization before Christ.

A few years later, Enki had ready his plan. He had already made contact through the phase with a woman called Mary who lived in Nazareth and had asked her in her dreams if she would accept to receive a child, who could become the Savior of humankind. Mary confused Enki with God since the stories among the Jews was God who talked with people through dreams. So she accepted.

Enki communicated the news to the Pleiadeans. So they asked for help to the Intraterrestrials, who took Maria in one of their ships while she slept and transferred her to the moon, where the Pleiadeans introduced her the genetic material that Enki had given them through artificial insemination and later returned her to the Earth.

Enlil, who was constantly spying on Enki, found out this plan and tried to stop it at all costs. However, on September 29th of 2 A. D, Jesus was born. And this event would change the future of humankind forever...

Jesus's War Declaration to Enlil

Enki, along with the Carians, created a human being very similar to the primordial, with thirty active codons in DNA; this would change the history of humankind completely. His name was Jesus.

While Enki carried out his plan, Enlil had already infiltrated many members of his chosen people in key positions to control Rome. And had created a vast Empire. When Enlil found out Enki's plan and heard him, in a conversation that he had with a Carian, immediately prevented this to happen. So he quickly contacted a hybrid, loyal to him, who was king of Rome and belonged to his chosen people and advised him to do everything to prevent this child from being born. Otherwise, he would put on risk all the Roman Kingdom. This king, called Herod, accepted the mission and agreed to kill all children under two years and that had been born in their territories.

Enki, upon finding this out, told Maria to escape. And while fleeing, in the town of Bethlehem, Jesus was born on September, 23 of 2 AD. To his birth, three Essenes magicians came to visit him, who were sent by Enki to help Joseph and Mary in their flee. These magicians led Mary, Joseph, and Jesus to Egypt to the White Brotherhood, which according to Enki, was the safest place where Jesus could be. Because during this time, this great Brotherhood of White magicians had not been detected by Enlil.

During the birth of Jesus and the flee from Egypt, Enki

did not have any contact with the Magi or Maria, since he was constantly guarded by Enlil. He had planned this much earlier. Because of this, he had sent the Essene magicians with precise instructions.

Herod thought that he had already killed the child and that he had fulfilled the mission entrusted by their God Yahweh. However, Enlil was not very convinced of this, so he suggested Herod to run a strict surveillance in the villages of Galilee, Nazareth, and Bethlehem, and if a child was born, he would inform him immediately.

Jose, Mary, and Jesus remained four years in the Great White Brotherhood of Egypt, until the death of Herod. Enlil, after all this time, suspected that the child had fled from the Roman Empire, but did not know where. Until one day, Enki, intentionally let Enlil overhear a conversation that he had with an Essene mage, in which he told him to protect a child in Egypt and then take him to Greece. Enlil, trusting in this conversation, began to contact all humans he had access to, and asked them to search for this child in Egypt and Greece.

Enki had tricked Enlil since he knew that the only place where he would not search was the place where they had escaped to, and when Herod had died, his vigilance had been forgotten. So, he advised Mary to return to her village, Nazareth. And they did so. Four-year-old Jesus lived in Nazareth as any other child. However, he realized very soon that he could modify reality with only thinking and pronouncing it. Since he was a child, he began to recognize his great power, however, he could not control it. Sometimes, when he was angered and thought of something bad, this also became reality.

Enki realized of the great potential that Jesus had. So

he decided to teach him, and there was no one better than the Essene magicians to do so. So he gave them precise instructions to teach Jesus.

It was until he was twelve, that the three Essene magicians went for him to instruct him in the Mission of the Christification of his conscience, and to dominate his power. He was first taken to the *Great White Brotherhood* in Egypt where he was trained for some years. Later, they took him to several secret lodges located in India, Tibet, Persia, Syria, and Greece; finally, he finished his training in Qumran, the village of the Essenes. They were surprised by everything that Jesus was able to do since he had reached a point at which he could change reality at will with only his words and thoughts.

Jesus during all his training understood all the manipulation to which humankind was exposed. And he understood exactly why the Kadistu made the decision to let the humans act on their own will. Jesus understood that he could not intervene directly in the awakening of the consciousness of humankind, but his mission was to show us the way to our awakening and freedom: humans must demonstrate that they are a breed worth of being preserved in the universe.

He also understood why Enki had devised this plan for the salvation of humankind. So he decided to cut off all communication with him to avoid being manipulated and began his journey to continue with his mission.

It should be noted that Enki could not contact Jesus, and understood very well that Jesus understood perfectly the law of free will, and did not want to be manipulated by anyone.

After finishing his training, Jesus was able to

communicate with the Universal source, THE TRUE GOD OF EVERYTHING, and Jesus referred to him as his father, since he understood that we are all One, since we are all Him.

Enki was surprised by the progress of Jesus, since it really scared him a little since no Anunnaki or Draconians in all their history had been able to communicate with *the Universal Source*.

It was at the age of thirty that Jesus returned to Nazareth to see Mary and Jose, and this is where he fully began to fulfill his mission. The first thing he did was to perform a ritual called baptism, in which he was helped by John the Baptist; a man who knew Jesus from childhood and who had been surprised by the miracles he had made and had been faithful to him since then. So, Jesus took him as his first disciple. In the baptism, Jesus was anointed and cleaned on his spirit.

Then he went to the desert where he was forty days fasting, and where he decided to contact Enlil to dissuade him from his plan of submitting the humankind. Enlil was surprised of the ease with which Jesus found him, he tried to tempt him, offering him pleasures, honors and riches of the Earth provided that he joined him into his plan to rule the world. Obviously, Jesus did not accept and warned him of the consequences of that.

Enlil realized he had to act quickly since Jesus was not a common human as the people he knew. He realized that he was special and could put an end to their plans if he didn't do something.

When Jesus returned from the desert, he went to Judea, where he formally declared war to Enlil throwing all the priests, preachers, desecrators, and sellers, out of the

Temple of Jehovah, alluding that who they adored was not God. Then was demonstrated that Jesus was against the Church and religion since he knew that was one of the most effective methods to control and manipulate humankind. He, then, returned to Galilee and met Maria Magdalena with which he fell in love and subsequently married in Canaan having two children, a man, and a woman.

Jesus was aware that to wake up humankind his work had to be written and recorded for posterity. So he chose his final twelve disciples, who followed him, listened to his words, and transcribed them witnessing his miracles.

It only took Jesus three years to make all kinds of miracles, which he carried out thanks to the faith that his followers had. The message of Jesus was very clear: *you create your own reality;* he only taught us the way.

Enlil was afraid of all that this man called Jesus was able to do. He quickly lost many followers of his chosen people, and they ceased to worship him. The only ones who followed him were hybrids that had Anunnaki blood, and most of them held positions of power. He tried by all means to contact people he had to stop Jesus. However, they did not accept since they feared Jesus and his miracles.

Enlil was contemplating the collapse of his power. Jesus was awakening the conscience of humankind and he could not do much. He had to wait for the hybrids to communicate with him through the agreed rituals, and it was there where contacted one who was a leader of the Pharisees telling him he had to stop Jesus at all costs. And so it was that they began to accuse him of conspiracy against the Roman Empire.

Jesus knew very well what was going to happen and the sacrifice that had to do. So, at the last supper, he made a ritual to give part of his power to his disciples and instructed them to spread the word and his deeds around the world over time. And he asked them help carry out his plan. He told Judas to handle him over so that he could fulfill his purpose.

Although Judas didn't want to do it, he did not disobey the commandment of his master. The Roman guard took Jesus to the Sanhedrin (Assembly or Council of elders of ancient Israel), but he could not be judged as they wanted. Since they didn't have the necessary civil powers. So Caiaphas, who was the hybrid contacted by Enlil, proposed that Jesus was brought before the Roman authorities, taking it before Pontius Pilate, who did not want to judge him, so he washed his hands and let the people decide whether they wanted to save him or Barabbas.

While Caiaphas had gotten a large number of Jews to vote against Jesus, in fact, they were not so many as to decide the future of the Nazarene, so Jesus changed the emotional frequency of the people gathered there to vote against him, and so he could carry out his sacrifice.

Enki did not understand very well the plan that Jesus had. How could he, sacrificing his life, save humankind? It was until later that he understood it.

Enlil knew that he was winning, but still had doubts, since, with the great power that Jesus had, it seemed very strange that everything was happening so quickly. Jesus was tortured and crucified on Mount Calvary. Just before he died, there was a total solar eclipse. And there, he contacted the Universal source and told it to forgive humankind, because they were not yet aware enough.

When his body was lowered from the cross, a soldier pierced him on one side of his body with a spear, and then they buried him in a grave covered with a large stone entrance.

Enlil was already victorious and also was completely bewildered by all that had happened. When suddenly, after three Earth days, Jesus resurrected and came before his Apostles showing Enlil and all the Anunnaki he had gotten *Christified* and had managed to overcome death. He gave the last instructions to his Apostles and said to his spouse, Mary Magdalene, to take their children to the *Great White Brotherhood*, where they would continue his work to balance the good and evil on Earth.

After this, Jesus ascended to the fifth dimension, overcoming the Draconians and reptilian Anunnaki being at the level of a Kadistu. Enlil was terrified with the power of Jesus and the work he had done on Earth. He knew that it was a matter of time for humankind to wake up. He had no choice but to ask for help from Anu and confessed to him that he and Enki could communicate with humans through the phase.

Anu, who had not been around Earth all this time, and did not understand any of this, agreed to help Enki; not out of interest, but for fear of losing the human farm and of the possibility of another Jesus that could deal with them. The truth was that Anu was no longer interested in the human Lulus since he had realized that he and all the other Anunnaki had become parasites of all human. They had left their lives behind becoming simple farmers controlled by the Draconians. In addition, he did not feel very much at home in the fourth dimension. So, he had been devising a plan to get rid of the Draconians control. He knew that his only option was to ask for help from his race Usumgal because if they joined the Kingu race, they could face the enormous power of the Draconians.

Meanwhile, the Draconians were not aware of what was happening on Earth until they realized that a human had managed to overcome them, and he had installed in the fifth dimension. They were bewildered and terrified by this event, so they decided to send a large caravan to the fourth dimension with the Anunnaki to see what was happening in Uras, Earth.

The Carians were impressed and had never imagined that a human could have so much power. On the one hand they were glad because humans were closer to their liberation, and on the other hand, they were aware that humans could represent a great danger if they increased their power and used it against them. So they began to doubt whether their plan was successful or not.

Enki, impressed, never thought at which level could Jesus get, and did not know if to regret or rejoice about this plan, since a human had overtaken them by far.

Finally, he realized that Jesus's mission had been a success: He had gotten Christified, he taught us the way to our liberation, and he had demonstrated all the alien races that the humans were a race to take into account, and that they were worth their existence in the universe.

But the most important thing is that Jesus had taught humankind was the most powerful force in the universe: *love.*

Anu and Enlil could not be idle. So, they started to devise a plan to revert this situation...

The God Yahweh and his New Identity

Reaching the fifth dimension, his disciples began to write and spread the story of Jesus, and this quickly spread throughout Rome and Europe.

This greatly reduced the number of believers of the god Yahweh and the Roman gods, reducing the chosen people to a minority and made staggering these religions.

[Margin note: False because Jews were always a minority at every at us time of Jesus]

Anu and Enlil, seeing that their power was crumbling, contacted their faithful disciples, the hybrids. They were the emperors of Rome and were advised to impose the polytheistic religion as the official, sentencing to death to whom did not profess it. [Margin note: imposing Christianity *]

It should be noted that Enlil was not entirely in agreement with this decision since he would have preferred Rome to put Yahweh as the one God. However, given the critical situation, he accepted and supported the decision. That is how it began in Rome the hunt of the followers of Jesus.

The second advice they gave to the hybrids was to chase and put an end to all the disciples of Jesus who spread his word to avoid them to be shared around the world. Each hybrid that was the Emperor took the advice, and they began to prosecute the disciples. However, the disciples had the support of the members of the society of *the White Dragon*, who knew very well that if they wanted humankind to be saved, it was necessary to share the message of Jesus, which was based on love and the destruction of dogmas and churches. Therefore, it was

[Bottom margin note: Christianity became aggressively dogmatic + the concept of LOVE was lost or diminished by dogma, unrelenting etc.]

very difficult to catch the disciples of Jesus to the Roman Empire.

While this was happening, the Draconians went to the fourth dimension and demanded an explanation from Anu, who told them that Jesus had been modified genetically by the Carians and the Pleiadeans, and that had caused all that disaster. The Draconians asked Anu why they did not have been advised before, and Anu replied that they had realized of that this until Jesus ascended into the fifth dimension.

The Draconians took this action of the Carians and Pleiadeans as a disobedience of the orders of the Kadistu since, for them, they had violated the law of free will of humans. So they decided to impose a complaint to the members of the Galactic Confederation.

Anu told them that they had already taken action in Uras, Earth, to reverse this and make a definitive break with the message of Jesus. But the Draconians were well aware that such measures would not work out, since the message of Jesus was going to survive through time and space, and advised Anu to change strategy: *they did not have to impose their polytheistic religion, but that they had to change the message of Jesus and persuade the humans of that. That is, make humans believe that Jesus gave a different message.*

Enlil who was listening to the conversation said it was going to take a long time, to which the Draconians answered that they had plenty of time.

Even though Anu had not told anything to the Draconians about the participation of Enki in the creation of Jesus, he put two security guards to watch Enki full-time so he did not come out of the fourth dimension and banned him from communicating with humans under penalty of banishment.

Enki, embarrassed with everything his plan had unleashed, was obliged to abide by the punishment of his father.

It was the year 60 AD, when Nero, a hybrid King of Rome, was commissioned to strictly comply orders from their Anunnaki masters. First, he attacked the town of Qumran, destroying almost entirely the Essenes, surviving only a dozen people who traveled to Egypt to take refuge in the White Brotherhood. Later in the year 67, Nero ordered the killing of Peter, and he was crucified head down in the circle of the Vatican Hill. He was buried there, in what we know today as the Vatican.

But Nero not only prosecuted the followers of Jesus but also hunted regularly the Jews, the chosen people of Enlil, destroying Jerusalem, since he wanted that the Roman religion was the only one. This marked the beginning of the *Diaspora or Dispersion of the Jews*, known as a wandering people and homeless.

Enlil could not stop the free will of Nero, so the only thing he could do was to contact a member of his chosen people, and advise him to flee with the greater number of people he could. He did this for the sole purpose of not wanting to lose his few worshipers on Earth.

However, despite all these murders and prosecution of the followers of Jesus, his words, teachings, and followers continued growing. Enlil realized that the Draconians were right. The message of Jesus was so strong that it could not be stopped, so he began to do the opposite of what Jesus preached.

Jesus did not want churches, so in the 69, Enlil advised Rome's new emperor, Vespasian, another hybrid to its service, to build a church in the name of Jesus, which would be in charge of the Roman Empire. Vespasian did not understand this advice since the prosecution of the followers of Jesus was at its peak. However, he decided to follow the advice of his god and put in charge to Linen, a man of his confidence, who was to become the first Pope in history.

Meanwhile, in the fourth dimension, the Anunnaki were monitored by a small number of the Draconians who had stayed there because the leaders went to make a formal complaint to the Galactic Confederation.

Anu was called to Orion by the Draconians to give his own words and tell the members of the Galactic Confederation what had happened with Jesus.

After he did this, Anu took this opportunity and on its return to the fourth dimension, he drifted his way and went in search of the Usumgal leaders to tell them all that the Draconians were doing. After listening to him, the Usumgal leaders brought a complaint to the reptilian Council, composed by the leaders of all reptilian races, since the Draconians had hidden information about the arrangements that were carried out in the Galactic Confederation and had not shared them with the reptilian Council, which was a serious violation of the reptilian laws.

The Draconians were called to trials and were dismissed from their post as representatives of the reptilian race in the Galactic Confederation.

The Draconians realized of the betrayal of Anu since he also spoke before the reptilian Council about everything that had happened with the Draconians. After several reptilian days, the reptilian Council did not come to an agreement and the Draconians declared war on the Usumgal, the Kingu, and Sutum since they did not want to lose the power they had in the Galactic Confederation. The only race that remained on the sidelines of this conflict was the Amasutum.

The fifth great reptilian war was about to begin. The Draconians knew that this war was not convenient, but they had no other choice if they did not want to lose their power before the Galactic Confederation and their human farm.

However, they had a hidden plan, because they knew since a long time ago, that to have power upon their farm in Uras, Earth, from the fourth dimension, was not the best thing, and even less with the law of free will. They knew that they were taking many risks and that they had to have representatives into the ground so that the manipulation would be more effective. So they implemented a plan they had been developing for some time, which was to modify the DNA of the Igigi —*grey ones*— so that they could resist the high densities of the Earth, and once finished they would create clones so that they could be sent to Earth... So they started with genetic experimentation on the grey ones, from a base in the satellite of Jupiter called Europe.

On Earth, was 213 AD, and little had changed: the followers of Jesus continued to increase and the power of Enlil was fading out.

The subtle energies of the humans were at their lowest levels. In addition, the Roman Empire was beginning to break down with countless revolts, showing the first signs of its decline.

Enlil had tried everything. He even had changed the

writings of the disciples of Jesus to convince people that he had no divine power. However, it did not work. People just took this new version of Jesus and then discarded it. In addition, the sons of Jesus who were the new leaders of the *Brotherhood of the White Dragon* had done a good job of spreading the word of Jesus. Enlil, by not being able to delete or change the writings of the disciples of Jesus, decided to change small passages making very subtle changes that were imperceptible to the read, but that would contribute to change the message of Jesus completely.

To this end, he found support in his hybrid, Constantine I, Emperor of Rome, which, in obedience to the advice of his god, put an end to the persecution of Christians with the *Edict of Milan*, promulgated during his mandate stipulating that it was no longer forbidden to read the Gospels; that is to say, the writings of the disciples of Jesus who narrated their story. In addition, Constantine commanded to build a great basilica on the burial of Peter and thus, it was formally born the Vatican.

The plan of Enlil was to give confidence to the followers of Jesus to begin to read his new modified gospels, and for that, he instructed Melquiades, Pope in charge of the church created by Rome to change various passages in the Gospels. For example: in the part which narrates that Jesus went to Judea to oust the priests, preachers, ghouls, and sellers from the temple of Jehovah, the words priests and preachers were eliminated, leaving the message that Jesus was not against the church nor Jehovah, but against the sellers in a sacred place. And so it was that Enlil came up with the worst idea to plunge humankind: *make humans believe that Jesus was the son of*

Jehovah.

And in every passage where it was mentioned that Jesus contacted the Universal Source, Enlil changed those words by *Father*, as many times as Jesus referred to the true God.

Enlil knew he could not put the name of Yahweh in the Gospels as it could be rejected, but putting the name of Father, this left open the possibility that Jesus had a real father. That was how the word of Jesus was deliberately manipulated.

However, there was still the most difficult part: to make people accept it. For that, he used the Popes and the new temple created by Rome, exclusive to the new followers of Jesus.

This new version of the story of Jesus had such small changes that people accepted it quickly as if it were the original, and being Enki out of communication with humans, he could not give notice to the Brotherhood of the *White Dragon* to stop this.

161 Earth years later, Enlil had already succeeded at making his modified Gospels be accepted by a large number of Christians, as the followers of Christ were baptized. And he also managed the church to be accepted, but more importantly, he managed to convince them that the father of Jesus was Yahweh. But he still couldn't totally connect these two stories. In addition, there were still many Christians who did not believe in the church and they did not have those gospels modified, and, to make things worse, he faced another big problem: *the Roman Empire had crumbled and it was coming to an end.*

Jesus was in the fifth dimension, he knew that he could not intervene directly in the free will of humans, however, he did not forget us. He devoted himself to see everything that was happening with our destiny. And at crucial moments in our history, he sent us from beyond clashes of conscious energies for our awakening. Seeing everything that had happened since the ascension of Jesus to the fifth dimension, the Galactic Confederation convened an urgent Assembly in an attempt to solve all the chaos that was happening in the galaxy with the reptilian war and the fear many alien races had of the power demonstrated by humans.

This Assembly had a double purpose since the Great Council of this Confederation had already planned a solution for the destiny of humankind that, if approved, would change our destiny forever and would open up the possibility for a Reptilian Pact...

The Pact of the Reptilian Beings

The fifth reptilian war was at its peak. This made the Draconians send a small contingent to the fourth dimension to take the Usumgal Anunnaki as prisoners and decide not to kill them. Because they controlled the phase, the more efficient way to communicate with the Lulus.

This was great news for Enki, because as a prisoner of war, he would be separated from the constant control of the Anunnaki guards that Anu had put on him. And despite the fact that the Usumgal Anunnaki had to strictly follow the instructions of the Draconians, he could take advantage of a neglect of them to try to fix things on Earth.

Enlil was really worried about their destiny and the other Anunnaki since he did not know how the Draconians would react if they lost the war against the Usumgal, Kingu, and Sutum alliance. They could most likely be executed. However, they were not in danger since the Draconians were very interested in getting the subtle energies of the human farm.

And the Anunnaki had acquired the ability to communicate with humans to manipulate them so as to maximize the recollection of subtle energies. On Earth it was 476 AD, when the Roman Empire fell into the hands of Odoacer, a warlord, a barbarian, who overthrew the young emperor Romulus Augustus and took over the government in Italy.

This was a harsh blow for the Anunnaki, since the

major recollection of negative energies came from the wars and rituals Romans did. This meant a considerable decrease in the energies emanated by humankind, since there were now left the isolated barbarian wars and the energies sent to the God Yahweh by people who believed in him. However, a great part of humankind believed in Jesus and that took away a lot of negative energy to the Anunnaki. So Enlil began to devise a plan to correct this: he had to connect more Jesus with Yahweh, and not leave it as his son.

In the shortage of negative energies, the Draconians ordered their Anunnaki prisoners to indoctrinate humans to worship many gods (as they did in past times), because their perception of it was that, the more gods the humans worshipped, the more subtle energies would emanate from them. This, did not benefit Enlil, since he was the most benefited by usurping the name of Yahweh as god. So he told the Draconians that was impossible because it would take a long time to indoctrinate all humans to believe in many gods again.

The Draconians told him that time was not a problem for them, since, compared to the time of the humans, they were eternal. So if they did not want to suffer the consequences, they had to comply with the orders and get to work.

Upon the threat of the Draconians, Enki proposed an idea: there were large settlements of humans that had not been indoctrinated throughout the American continent. They could manipulate them as they had done it in Egypt and Sumeria. The Draconians accepted this idea and told him that they wanted to possess those Lulus, and they also wanted blood sacrifices in his honor. Therefore, the

Anunnaki turned towards Mesoamerican civilizations that had already achieved great advances without the help of the extraterrestrial gods.

Although Enki took that decision to save his Anunnaki fellows, he knew that these humans in America came from Atlantis and they were more intelligent and less manipulable than their Egyptian or Sumerian predecessors. So he told the Draconians that in order to get that, they needed technology and knowledge, otherwise it could not to be possible. The Draconians told him that it did no matter what he did, they wanted results.

This was a great opportunity for Enki. He could finally try to amend his error.

Enlil, surprised by this race of humans that had no knowledge, saw in it an opportunity to be the only god, and before starting with the manipulation in America, he decided to continue with the Roman Empire. As for him, that empire had to be an example of how humans should be indoctrinated. So he contacted Simplicio, a hybrid faithful to him and that served as the Pope at that time, and ordered him to continue practicing the rituals of blood and the laws of the Roman Empire, but now hidden from the seat of the Vatican.

Obviously, Simplicio and the other popes, followed this order. And in this way the Roman Empire continued their domains, camouflaged now from the Vatican.

It took only one hundred Earth years to the Anunnaki to indoctrinate the Mesoamericans, and they created great civilizations, pyramids in strategic points of the Earth to maximize the subtle energies, in addition to teaching them the art of war and sacrifices.

They focused on the areas of the South and Central

America. And they achieved this so fast thanks to the advice of Enki, since in exchange of technologies and knowledge, the leaders of these civilizations agreed to do the rituals of blood. Thus were born civilizations such as the Mayas and Incas. To the latter (precisely the settlers of the Nazca culture), they taught to make enormous drawings on Earth so that only the icons could be seen from above, as that is the perspective they have from the fourth dimension; and they did this because the Draconians liked these drawings. That is to say, they had hundreds of men doing these lines in the Nazca region, just for the Draconian's fun.

Enki took advantage of that distraction to communicate with humans and he began to teach the Mayas prohibited knowledge about astrology, mathematics and time. He wanted to amend his error because he felt guilty that the only free humans now had already been indoctrinated, and he realized that in order to evolve, as Jesus did, he had to detach from his ego and help humankind, not for his benefit, but for the benefit of others. From that moment on, Enki stopped seeing humankind as his creation and began to respect them.

The Draconians were surprised by the great advance of these civilizations, but especially of the Mayas, as they had mastered the Mathematics, Agriculture, Astrology, and had managed to understand the time like no other human race. They even began to understand time lines and how to anticipate them, something that the Draconian race was beginning to understand. They realized that the human race was a species to be feared.

In the meantime, the Intraterrestrials had already developed their technology and had already studied the human being; they discovered that this species had not evolved because their pineal gland was disconnected and they suspected that if humans activated it, they could be a great threat to them. They constantly came out of the Abzu and monitored the Earth in their cigar-shaped ships. They had even already begun to explore other planets, thanks to the technology inherited by the Anunnaki. They began to have contact with a human settlement in the north of America, in what is now the United States, and began to tell them how they had been manipulated with genetical engineering by some beings who had come from Orion. In addition, they taught them to respect nature and to live in harmony with the planet.

Many of these beings, were invited to the Abzu to live with them. This human settlement is what we know as the Hopi Indians, and that is the reason why this group of humans had no large constructions and perfectly knew the origin of the human being.

The Galactic Confederation had convened an urgent meeting for the year 600 AD, approximately, Earth time. But it could not be carried out because the reptilian races did not attend due to a boycott that the Draconians made to the Usumgal. So, after mediating with all the Reptilian races, they managed to hold an Assembly around the year 940 AD, Earth time.

This was the first meeting to which the Intraterrestrials were invited, since they would play a crucial role in the plan that the leaders of the Galactic Confederation had. They exposed in this council that due to what happened to Jesus, humans had to be controlled in one way or another, without affecting their free will. So they proposed to use the planet Earth as a planet of test for the *incarnated souls.* This meant that the Earth was going to become a host for souls of different beings that, in order to evolve, had to go through a very difficult test on a planet with very high density. This test would also apply to humans and would serve as a final test to know if this species was worth of evolving into higher dimensions.

This type of planets existed in different galaxies and were occupied as a final test for species that were stuck in their evolution and needed a final exam to demonstrate if they were worthy to evolve, if they did not pass the test, these species were condemned to repeat their life on that planet with high density. In that they wanted to transform planet Earth...

This resulted in a great debate among all species of the Galactic Confederation, since many were in favor and others against. And this was a great opportunity that the Draconians took advantage of, since they argued that if this was done, it was going to be very easy for humans and for embodied souls of other beings, because the density of the Earth was not as high as the planets used for final tests, and this would not represent a test itself. So they proposed to keep with the human control and put tests increasingly difficult. So they could check whether the Lulu humans were a species that was worth it or not. They wanted to go back to Earth to become gods as in the past.

The leaders of the Galactic Confederation said that was part of their plan: to let the Reptilians continue in control of humankind without any hindrance, but as they were currently doing it from the fourth dimension, without direct intervention with humans in order not to violate their free will.

This would imply that the Intraterrestrials would have

to be respected, and no race could go to the Abzu, unless they wanted to. That is to say, this could only apply to humans and reincarnated souls which would have to possess only human bodies.

After much debate and many arguments that the leaders of the Galactic Confederation dealt with, this proposal was approved in its majority by the extraterrestrial races that feared humans for what happened with Jesus.

It should be noted that the Carians, the Pleiadeans, and Andromedans voted against it, because for them this was going against the resolution of the Kadistu. In the face of defeat, the Carians proposed to the General Assembly to take the most advanced humans on Earth at that time, and move them to the Abzu of Mars to continue their evolution without any type of manipulation, and, in that way, see how they freely evolved.

This was approved by a majority of extraterrestrial races that wanted to clean up a little their karma with the exception of the Reptilians who voted against it.

The Carians also invited the Intraterrestrials to the Abzu of Mars because it was uninhabited and, in that way, they could live in a larger planet coexisting with the humans that were moved there, and be out of all the manipulation that there would be on the surface of the Earth.

The Draconians were the most benefited from this decision, since they would be able to control their human farm without the obstacle of any extraterrestrial race.

And thus, it was born the Reptilian Pact, where the Draconians negotiated to share the spoils of the Earth with the Usumgal Anunnaki, and agreed to return a farm planet to the Kingu, which had been snatched away from them a long time ago. In exchange for ending the reptilian war.

In addition they came to the agreement that there was going to be a representative of the Kingu, two of the Draconians, and one of the Sutum at the Galactic Confederation.

In this same pact, they agreed with the Galactic Confederation that the Reptilians could not attack for any reason Mars, they could not enter the Abzu of Earth, they could not put at risk the existence of the human race, they could not mess with the Intraterrestrials, and in addition, they would leave the Pleiadeans as the only race that could control the Moon, among many other agreements.

This reptilian pact was going to change the history of humankind forever, and was going to place it in its darkest moment. And it would be the greatest test that we would have to deal with as humans. However, Jesus had already had foreseen all of this…

Enlil's Big Fraud

When it was decided that the Earth would become a planet for testing the souls stuck in their evolution, this made the opportunity for the Reptilian Pact in which the Draconians agreed to share the subtle energies of humankind with the Anunnaki. Obviously, the most benefited with this were the Draconians, since they only had to pick up the subtle energies, while the Usumgal Anunnaki had to contact the Lulu humans to collect these negative energies, for which Anu demanded the Draconians to let him manipulate humankind at their will without their intervention to maximize these negative energies which would be shared between the two races.

The Draconians accepted and let the Anunnaki manipulate humankind at their will, because they had a hidden plan, since the Igigi, grey ones, who had been cloned in the moon of Jupiter, had passed the test of resistance of density and were ready to tolerate the Earth's atmosphere. With them, the Draconians could manipulate and study humans, as they were very interested in how their feelings worked, something that very few extraterrestrial races had, and no one had at our level. That makes us special in the universe because we are the only species able to express feelings at that level.

So they started to send these grey ones in a flying saucer, to begin with their mission. This deal of letting the Anunnaki freely manipulate humankind was the best opportunity that Enlil would have had to carry out his plan of becoming the only god of Earth, so he told his plan to Anu: Enlil wanted to expand his modified gospels, now, in the new continent so they would leave their polytheistic beliefs and be transformed into faithful followers of Yahweh.

Anu vehemently opposed to that, as the negative energies had increased thanks to the sacrifices and the beliefs of the Mesoamerican civilizations, so he wanted to continue like that as well. In addition, Anu told Enlil that by spreading the modified gospels, many people would send their energies to Jesus as the Son of Yahweh. And that would lower the uptake of energy. He suggested him to solve that problem before making any plan.

Enlil, annoyed by his father's decision, knew deep down that he was right because when putting together the story of Yahweh with the one of Jesus, and passing him as his son, many people would start to believe in Yahweh, but they would also believe in Jesus. And the energy would be divided in two, and this was not convenient for the Anunnaki.

Meanwhile, a group of Carians went to the Moon to ask the Pleiadeans what was the most advanced human race in those moments on Earth, according to their observations. The Pleiadeans replied that the Mesoamerican civilizations had an incredible potential, and were the fittest to be transferred to Mars and saved from the future manipulation.

Subsequently, the Carians went to Enki and asked his opinion in this regard. Enki said that the civilization that should be saved and transferred to Mars was the Mayas. The Carians held Enki to that and told him to communicate with the Mayas to ask them if they wanted to be saved and transferred to Mars. Enki communicated with the Mayas. In addition, he told them that they had been chosen to be saved.

The Maya leaders took this as a prophecy from their gods. So they asked the people if they wanted to be transferred out of the Earth. The vast majority agreed, and so it was that, from one day to the next, the Carians took the Maya, in a huge ship, along with eighty percent of the Intraterrestrials towards the Abzu of Mars. The other twenty percent of the remaining Intraterrestrials decided to stay in the Abzu of the Earth to preserve their home and continue studying humans. In addition, they already had the technology to reach Mars without problems.

Once they took out the Mayas and part of the Intraterrestrials from Earth, the Draconians started to work, and led the first grey ones to the region of Asia, since that was the part of the world that was less indoctrinated. Although the first gospels started to arrive, it was not yet defined their belief system. So the Draconians instructed the Igigi, *grey ones*, to communicate with the leaders of those regions and teach them a belief system totally different from those established by the Anunnaki.

And in the regions of the Middle East, who had begun to be indoctrinated with the Gospels, they began to change the name of the God Yahweh and Jesus. And it was this as they began to use names such as Zoroaster, Mohammed, Allah, etc. This was with the purpose for humankind not to worship only Yahweh, since that gave power to Enlil and allowed him to live double the time on average his race lived, which the Draconians tried to avoid at all costs. Obviously at the back of the Anunnaki in order not to look suspicious.

In the meantime, Enki contacted the members of the

White Brotherhood, and proposed them to expand all over the world; that is to say, to create more brotherhoods around the world to try to stop all the manipulation that was coming.

It should be noted that the leaders of the White Brotherhood were the lineage of Jesus, who, following the teachings of their master, did not have any communication with the Anunnaki to avoid being manipulated. However, several members of the brotherhood could contact Enki through the phase and informed them about his proposal for expansion. The lineage of Jesus had already thought of expanding. And they decided it was a good idea due to the resolution that the Galactic Confederation had taken on turning the planet into a difficult test for humans.

So they started the expansion of this brotherhood, attracting more and more followers, and camouflaging with different names all over the planet in order not to be detected by the Anunnaki, all with the sole purpose of awakening humankind and to promote their evolution.

On the other hand, Anu, who was appointed by the Usumgal as the leader of their human farm, devoted himself to direct and coordinate the farm. He finally had the freedom to leave the fourth dimension and return when he wanted to. And, worried by the power that Jesus still had on Earth, he came up with an absurd idea, but if it worked out, it would diminish the influence of Jesus on Earth and multiply the negative energy captured by the Anunnaki.

Anu told Enlil to pass Yahweh as Jesus himself. Which meant the following: to merge them into a single person and not pass him as simply his son. Enlil, initially rejected the idea because the human indoctrination was already too advanced to make them believe at that point that Jesus was not the son of Yahweh, but Yahweh himself. Anu told him to find the way to do it, since by doing it, they would get great benefits, since people, while thinking of Jesus, would automatically think in Yahweh and all energies would be transferred to him.

After several Earth years thinking on this idea, Anu and Enlil, came to the conclusion that it was easier to say that the God Yahweh can do everything, and this is why he came to the Earth incarnated as his own son named Jesus. Enlil had many doubts about this because he did not believe that humankind was so innocent to believe that story.

Anu, fearing that this idea could not work, asked Enlil to divide this God into three persons and not in two, since Anu wanted to capture part of that energy and take power from his son. Thus, it was born the idea that God is divided into Father, Son, and Holy Spirit. The Holy Trinity. And they used all of their hybrids, and especially the Vatican, to try to put this new idea in the humans established in the European continent.

200 Earth years had passed by, and few things had changed on Earth. In America, the Mesoamerican cultures were still making sacrifices and wars in the name of their gods. In Asia, in what we now know as India and China, they began to be indoctrinated with new polytheistic ideas. In the Middle East, the teachings of the gospels were refuted and people there began to worship no longer Yahweh, but other gods with different names. And finally, in Europe, the idea that Yahweh is Jesus had not been accepted by people. No matter how much propaganda

and changes in the gospel the Vatican did, humankind rejected this idea.

The power of Enlil, Yahweh, had declined dramatically although the negative energy remained stable. This terribly worried Enlil. So in a desperate act in 1184 AD, he instructed a hybrid, Pope Innocent III, head of the Vatican in that moment, to create a crusade in union with all the churches to prosecute and punish under penalty of death those who would not accept the idea that Yahweh and Jesus were the same. And that was the beginning of the Holy Inquisition, which condemned as heretics, witches, and shamans, to all the people who would not accept that Jesus and Yahweh were the same person. After some time, the Vatican practically had an army to hunt heretics and impose their idea.

At the beginning, Anu opposed to this idea, but seeing that the massacres and torture generated by this anti-heretics crusade generated a lot of negative energy, he let Enlil continue with his plan.

Enki could not believe what was happening on Earth, and although the White Brotherhood had saved many lives, he could never equal the army of the Vatican. Without any doubts, Enlil had taken an advantage out of reach.

While this was happening, the grey ones continued with their investigations and indoctrination at the back of the Anunnaki until on one occasion, the flying saucers were detected by several cigar-shaped ships of the Intraterrestrials, which, upon the ignorance of these ships and the fear of an unknown alien race invasion, did not hesitate to shoot them, and a battle started in the sky, which many people were able to witness at first sight, and which was set forth in paintings and books for posterity.

The Anunnaki, having realized of this battle, discovered that the Igigi were manipulating the beliefs of Asians, so Anu decided to put a complaint to the Galactic Confederation.

Upon the defeat of the Igigi against the Intraterrestrials and the threat of Anu to file a complaint to the Galactic Confederation, the Draconians decided to accept that they were the ones who had sent the grey ones, but simply to observe and study humans, without altering their free will, as the Intraterrestrials did. And managed to agree that the Igigi could continue with their studies, although the Anunnaki and Intraterrestrials did not trust the Draconians, they decided not to get into trouble with them and did not report anything to the Galactic Confederation.

Almost three hundred years after the imposition of the Holy Inquisition had passed, and it was beginning to produce its benefits. The belief that Jesus and Yahweh were the same person, was already rooted in Europe, and this had strengthened again Enlil. It had positioned him as a powerful deity on Earth.

Without any doubt, it had been a success. Only something was missing, the expansion of this idea all over the world...

The Origin of the Jesuits

When Anu and Enlil were able to implant the idea that Jesus was Yahweh himself, through the Holy Inquisition, this added a big amount of energy to Enlil. However, he wanted more. The wanted to be the God of the whole world. So he began to devise a plan to achieve it.

Anu, seeing that Enlil became increasingly powerful, decided to ask for help from one of his Anunnaki subjects who dominated the phase to communicate with humans at the back of Enlil, because his plan was to acquire the same power as him.

For their part, the White Brotherhood had already expanded to various parts of America, Asia, and Africa, creating secret lodges that aimed to raise awareness, consciousness, and the human spirit out of all religious dogma. That is why the apprentices called their master *builders*.

The original idea of Enki to create these lodges was to serve as an obstacle to any plan that would jeopardize the awakening of the conscience of humankind.

The Draconians, seeing that the negative energies coming from the European continent had decreased after the end of the Holy Inquisition, demanded the Usumgal Anunnaki to increase the recollection of the energy so that they would be at the same level of that of the American continent. On this pressure, Anu ordered Enlil to manipulate the humans of the European continent to start a war.

Enlil, annoyed with this idea, because he had to delay his personal plans, began to contact through the phase with a girl who was not a hybrid because he wanted to use their hybrids for his own interests. So, he established contact with this pure human and began to manipulate her to such a degree that he led her to lead one of the largest armies of those times. The name of this girl was Joan of Arc, who, carrying out all his battles, she believed that the voice she heard in her own dreams, was that of God himself, who gave her orders and guided her in his war.

With these clashes, Enlil managed to appease the demands of the Draconians and took advantage of, in secret, to put his plan on action to indoctrinate the entire American continent using his hybrids, the kings of Spain, to seek a man to sail their boats to the American continent. A continent unexplored and new to them, on the promise that those territories would be exploited and ruled by them. The only thing he asked was to take the modified gospels and religious beliefs to this new world.

The Spanish kings, believing faithfully in the promises of their god, saw in Christopher Columbus the right person to make this journey. And so it was that in 1492, Columbus arrived in America following the path indicated by the kings, with the sole purpose of appropriating all the natural resources of this new continent, and indoctrinate all people to believe in Yahweh, the one God in the world.

It is worth mentioning that Enki, years before of the discovery of this new continent by the Europeans, tried to warn the Mesoamerican cultures to prepare for this meeting, and not to be manipulated. Since Enki had listened to a conversation in which Enlil revealed this plan to Anu. These warnings of Enki were taken as prophecies that unfortunately occurred in 1492.

Enlil knew that the conquest and indoctrination of America would cost a lot of time and effort, so he decided to act fast. He ordered his hybrids, the kings, to send armies to seize the territories and propagate their religion. The Kings, always obedient, sent an army led by Hernan Cortes.

After almost thirty years of battles, Enlil realized that the Mesoamericans, in spite of not having the technology the Europeans had, were very intelligent and did not surrender so easily. Even more, the casualties of the Spain army were so many that he foresaw an imminent defeat. Desperate, he contacted a leader of the Spanish army and gave him instructions to create bacteriological diseases, implanting viruses such as smallpox, measles, influenza, the bubonic plague, diphtheria, typhoid fever, scarlet fever, chicken pox, yellow fever, etc., so that they would spread silently between the indigenous and ensure victory. It should be noted that he also gave him the vaccines for the Spanish Army to resist these diseases.

With this act, the balance started leaning in his favor. And he got the Spaniards to take an advantage out of reach.

Anu, seeing this move of Enlil, began to accelerate his plans to diminish his power. In addition, he had already discovered that Enki, was in contact with a group of people who followed the teachings of Jesus, and had created secret societies, imperceptible to the Anunnaki domain to put obstacles in their plans. So he decided to kill two birds with one stone, his plan was to: Create a secret society that would manipulate governments and world religions from the shadows and, thus, to be able to make decisions that would benefit him. In addition, he wanted to destroy the lodges of the White Brotherhood, which were helped by Enki.

So in 1540, almost 50 years after the new world, Anu decided it was time to put his plan on action. And informed a man who had the gift of listening to them, and to whom they had already tested some time ago. This man was Ignatius of Loyola, a Spanish military and religious fanatic, characterized mainly by their devotion to the Catholic Church, and by absolute obedience to the Pope. This man easily manipulable was influenced to create a secret society called *"The Company of Jesus"* on September, 27 of 1540; all in the name of his god. What is curious is that the statutes of this company, designed by Anu himself, and handed over to Loyola, considered the infiltration within other secret lodges for their destruction or seizure from the inside. In addition to seizing the power of governments, through infiltration and espionage.

With this, Anu tried to seize the secret lodges of the White Brotherhood, which at that time were already known as Freemasonry and which had grown rapidly around the world, and thus, tried to curb their power, in addition to infiltrate the largest number of people in governments and religions to manipulate them from the shadows. This *company* of Jesus had the blessing of the Pope himself, and was soon known as the Jesuits and spread like a *cancer* within the Masonic and European governments, getting great power in very little time. This master move granted him control over the human Lulus, Enlil, and Enki without realizing it.

While this was happening, European governments like France and Portugal, upon knowing of the new continent, they began to send troops to try to stay with a piece of the pie. This actually was of no interest to Enlil, as his sole purpose was to indoctrinate the Mesoamericans, and those countries also preached the gospels modified by Enlil.

The Draconians worried that their captured energy could decrease by everything that was happening in Uras, Earth, told Anu that they did not agree that humans had only one God since that would lower their negative energy. Anu told them they had to respect the free will of humans. And that would ensure that the negative energy remained constant.

The Draconians suspected that the Usumgal Anunnaki had influenced this to happen, so they decided to focus on the Asian countries that were more populated and sent more grey ones in their flying saucers to accelerate the indoctrination of these people in religions that were totally different from those promulgated by Enlil.

It took almost two hundred years for the indoctrination of America to be achieved, and they turned from a polytheistic religion to a monotheistic one, taking Yahweh as maximum God. Although it should be noted that, due to the mixture of these two religions, humans also began to worship saints and virgins of all kinds. Something that did not bother Enlil, as long as they deemed Yahweh as the maximum god.

The secret societies of the White Brotherhood were the only ones which stayed out of this indoctrination, and faithfully followed the teachings of Jesus.

Enki had already realized that something strange was going on in the lodges of Europe since several times they had made decisions that did not stick to the teachings of

Jesus, though he did not suspect that the Jesuits, the order created by Ignatius of Loyola, were behind all of this.

Jesus, seeing that humankind began again to decrease their vibrational frequencies got ready to send the first *wave of consciousness* from the fifth dimension...

The Origin of Illuminati

At the beginning of 1700, the Jesuits had already infiltrated into the vast majority of Masonic lodges in Europe changing their precepts of equality for following their own interests, or better said, the interests of Anu. The only remaining free lodges were the lodges in Asia, South America, and the Great Lodge of Egypt, which kept at the tight seal to new followers.

Enki knew something was wrong because his instructions were not observed by the European lodges, and had realized that they did not follow the precepts of Jesus, but now they performed strange occultist rituals. He sensed that Anu or Enlil had put their hand on them. So he decided to investigate what had happened.

Enlil, realized that his Chosen People, the Zionist Jews, were less and less, because they were treated as a minority in Europe, and roamed from country to country without any success. This caused many adherents to drop out and believe in other religions such as the Catholic one. This, although in reality did not affect much Enlil, due to the fact that he controlled these two religions, was an alert for him, as he needed a group of humans totally faithful to him to continue with his plans. So he decided to carry on with the promise he had made hundreds of years before and gave them the secret of power: the economic power in the world.

Enlil contacted the Zionist leaders and told them that in order to gain the economic power of the world and grow as the Chosen People, they only had to follow a rule: lend money without interest or fixed term to all Zionists that needed it, and when they had the possibility to pay, they would have to do it. With this simple rule, the Zionists began to run countless businesses, and in a very short time, they managed to have large amounts of money, which they took advantage of to make loans to people who were not Jewish, charging an interest for this. The first bankers had come to light.

It is amazing that, by following this simple rule of their God, Yahweh, Zionist Jews had obtained the economic power in the world today.

Seeing all the chaos that there was on Earth and that the evolution was totally paralyzed, Jesus decided to send a shock wave of consciousness from the fifth dimension. So he contacted the Pleiadeans and the Carians so that they could project this *shock wave* and spread it all over the Earth.

The Pleiadeans, with the help of the Carians, used the Moon to store all this energy and subsequently spread it on the Earth in doses that were digestible for humans. This led to a cultural and intellectual movement throughout the world, which would help humankind to advance and promote their evolution.

The Pleiadeans began to spread this clash of conscience in the European continent, and in the middle of the 17th century, it was born the *Illustration or Century of the Gods*, named in this way for its declared objective *to dispel the darkness from humankind through the lights of reason.*

At this time, thanks to the Conscious Shock, sent by Jesus, great thinkers, and inventors who believed in the idea that human knowledge could combat ignorance, superstition, and tyranny, to build a better world were born.

The *Illustration* had a great influence on the scientific, economic, political, and social aspects at that time. Anu, Enlil, and Enki himself were surprised by all the advances in the technology, social and political system that the European continent had reached, and they suspected that the human Lulus were being helped in some way by the Pleiadeans.

Enki saw in this situation an opportunity to take power from the human hybrids, faithful to Enlil, who served as kings in the European continent, and instructed the Masonic lodges to get ready to create several revolutions and, thus, definitely deprive kings of power.

Anu, upon noticing the plans of Enki, decided to support him with his Jesuits infiltrators, since one of the goals of Anu was to take power away from Enlil, and he knew that by taking away the power of the kings, Enlil would feel decimated, and would open a window of opportunity for Anu to get the power of the European continent. However, he knew that in order to achieve this, he did not only have to have the Jesuits infiltrated in most of the Masonic lodges, but he had to control a masonic society himself. So, he instructed his subject Anunnaki to convince a Jesuit to create a secret society under the rituals and precepts of Anu.

This Anunnaki subject got in contact with a German Jesuit of Jewish origin named Johann Adam Weishaupt, who, following the orders of his god, managed to convince the German banker, Mayer Amschel Bauer, best known as the founder of the Rothschild dynasty, to finance a secret society that would have as main objectives: the creation of a world government with a single religion, a single currency, the prohibition of private property, and the abolition of all monarchies. And so it was that the first of May, 1776, in the middle of the *Night of Walpurgis (pagan festivity on the night of April 30 to May 1 by large regions of Central and Northern Europe)*, was born the order of the Illuminati of Bavaria, which afterward would be known as the Illuminati.

This would be the first Masonic lodge outside of any influence of Enki and the Brotherhood of the White Dragon. This was totally controlled by Anu.

Enki, who was unaware of all these plans of Anu and Enlil, by chance, he found out all of this, since a lightning bolt struck one of the messengers of Weishaupt and the Government of Bavaria realized that this secret society planned to abolish all the monarchies of the world and overtake the power the kings, so Enlil decided to take matters into his own hands, and instructed the Catholic Church and the Government of Bavaria, and after that, all Europe, to prohibit and chase down the organization of the Illuminati and all secret societies that existed.

This witch-hunt lasted until 1785 when this society "supposedly" faded away completely. Something that was not true, since Anu, after realizing that he could not beat the power of the governments and the Catholic Church under the control of Enlil, decided to deceive him, and move the last of the members of the Illuminati to the new continent, specifically to the United States, which, later, would become the last world empire.

Enki seeing this persecution of the secret societies decided to accelerate his plans. And using the Masonic lodges, started the French Revolution in 1789, a social and political conflict with various periods of violence that destabilized France and sought the abolition of the monarchy, which would end up years later with the coup d'état of Napoleon Bonaparte in 1799, who would be controlled afterward by Enlil…

Enki's First Great Victory

With the birth of the Illuminati and the persecution and destruction of the secret societies thanks to Enlil, Enki took advantage of this to mobilize the freemasonry in America and promote the great revolutions that would generate the independence of the American countries, getting rid once and for all, of the oppression exerted by the European countries on them.

Enki knew it was the perfect time, since the shock wave sent by Jesus not only led to the Enlightenment and the technological and scientific progress of humankind, but also inspired the human community a sense of justice and freedom, and he had to take advantage of it, and so did it: starting with the United States where the human Lulus fought for their freedom in a long lasting conflict.

Obviously Enlil was not going to allow him to take this country out of its control. So, he sent several troops from their most powerful countries, but due to the distance and the enormous cost to send troops by sea, he was not able to preserve that country, and on July 4, 1776, the United States became independent from the British Empire.

Enlil was worried, because, with this defeat, he had lost his power in America, while in Europe things were not going better, since in France, conflict and violent manifestations were growing day by day; and that, coupled with the war victories of the mason, Napoleon Bonaparte, put him in a difficult situation.

Anu took advantage of the independence of the United

States and Enlil's distraction, and transferred the surviving members of his secret society, the Illuminati of Bavaria, who lived hidden in Europe to the new free country of America. The ancestors of the Illuminati went to America at the end of 1700. Their purpose was to start the infiltration in Freemasonry to control it from within and so stop the progress of Enki to create a fairer and free place.

In the year 1799, Napoleon Bonaparte made a coup d'État in France, causing a harsh blow to Enlil, who was watching his power rapidly declining. He had learned two very important things with this defeat: the first was that the conspiracy and organization through secret societies were fundamental to get power or take it away from their holder; and the second learnt lesson was that human Lulus were not so easy to enslave. He recalled thousands of years ago, a Lulu attacked a hybrid causing a revolution and awakening in those times.

Enlil, desperate, asked Anu for help, proposing to create a secret society to help diminish the power of his brother Enki, and stop his plans. Anu replied that thanks to his stupid decision of destroying all the secret societies in Europe, he could not help him. However, Anu said that he would take care of the American continent, and the only thing that Enlil had to worry about was to regain power in Europe.

It should be emphasized that Anu did not say at that moment that, in reality, he continued to control the Jesuits and Illuminati, because he wanted to use them not only to stop to Enki, but also to seize Enlil's power from the shadow.

At the refusal of his father, Enlil planned to create a

secret society with the most faithful members of his chosen people, however, this plan was postponed because, unexpectedly, when entering phase, and establishing communication with one of his followers, he discovered that Napoleon Bonaparte, although he did not dominate the phase, he could get into it through his dreams. It was then, that he decided to manipulate him by putting on him ideas of power. Little by little he realized that his plan worked because Napoleon had a big ego and that made him someone easily influenced.

The achievement of Enlil was to convince him to create a world empire and, in little more than a decade, Napoleon managed to take control of almost the entire Western and Central Europe, through a series of conquests and alliances. This increased the power of Enlil, and the negative energy captured for the Draconians.

Enki, seeing the betrayal of Napoleon, realized that his followers and members of the White Brotherhood, the White Dragon, and Masonry, were also impressionable and could change sides at any time. So, from that moment on, he instructed the brotherhood of the White Dragon to remain totally sealed and closed to new members, leaving the door only open to initiates who inherited the right to a place there, for example: children or relatives or people who, by their acts to humankind, would earn their place with an invitation. Since that moment, the Brotherhood of the White Dragon became the most secret society all over the world.

But if the ego of Napoleon led him to conquer almost all of Europe, it was also his ego what led him to lose his empire, since, feeling protected by his god who communicated with him in dreams, he thought himself invincible. However, his losses in Leipzig in October 1813 and Waterloo, in Belgium, on 18 July 1815, marked his exile to the island of St. Helena where he died in absolute solitude.

Enlil learned a third lesson with the defeat of Napoleon: he realized that the human Lulus were capable of doing anything for power, even kill and exterminate their own species. That was something that he was going to take advantage of from now on.

The Draconians were still using the grey ones to study humans, and had already realized that a small amount of mutated Lulus had a gene in the brain that made them smarter, cold and calculating, unable to feel affection for another human being. The humans were more similar to the Reptilians than the mammals.

They also discovered that they were easily traceable, as they always had negative blood ORH. These humans are the ones that we know nowadays as psychopaths.

The Draconians were more and more surprised with the things humans were capable of transmitting through their feelings. However, ha had not yet found the key to be able to transfer that feature to the reptilian race. However, this discovery could help them increase the energy collected on their farm. So they decided to pass such information to Anu for him to look for those Lulus with negative blood ORH and so that they could be manipulated more easily.

This information was perfectly suitable for Anu, because this gave him a definite advantage against Enlil.

Enki decided to accelerate his plans for the liberation of America and, using the masonry that still was not influenced by the Jesuits, he achieved the independence of Mexico, started on September 16, 1810, by the Cry of Dolores *(considered the act with which the war of Independence of Mexico started. According to the tradition, it consisted in the call to arms that the priest Miguel Hidalgo y Costilla, in the company of Ignacio Allende, Juan Aldama, made to his followers against New Spain)* that the mason Miguel Hidalgo gave and culminated with the entrance of the Army to Mexico City on 27 September 1821.

Enki continued releasing all South America using freemasons as Simon Bolívar to take the power from the Spanish, English and French empires, and thus, restore freedom to the American continent. Of course, Enlil was not going to let this last for a long time.

The Galactic Confederation, for its part, totally forgot the planet Uras, Earth, since they only regarded it as another prison planet. Where, by the way, the thousand five hundred souls incarnated on the Earth had not been able to get out of it, what reassured them that the Earth was the most difficult test planet of all they had in their possession. Although the Confederation had forgotten the Earth, it was constantly monitored from the Moon, as they feared that another Jesus came up. That is why they granted the control to the Draconians so that it does not happen again.

On Earth it was 1830 AD, and the shock wave of awareness that Jesus had sent from the fifth dimension was about to come to an end, and this concerned Enki, since, despite the progress made by humankind, they were not aware enough to achieve their true freedom. In addition, he knew that Enlil and Anu were planning something to regain all their power…

The Beautiful Dream of Tesla

Anu took advantage of the infiltration through his followers, the Jesuits in Freemasonry to corrupt it and control it from within. In addition, he commissioned them to infiltrate into the Illuminati of Bavaria, from Europe in positions of power of the new American government to seize it.

In the meantime, Enlil, led his Chosen People, the Zionists, to get the economic power of all Europe, by controlling the banking and commerce in general of all that area, led of course by the *Rothschild dynasty*.

The wave of awareness sent by Jesus was extended to the beginning of 1900 when it would finally end. This would be exploited by Anu and Enlil to start an era of darkness manipulated by them, since they knew that Jesus would take approximately one hundred Earth years to send the next shock wave of awareness; however, just before the end of this shock wave on Earth, there were born great geniuses that would completely change the history of humankind, and precisely on July 10, 1856, it was born one of the brightest minds that has lived in this planet, his name, Nikola Tesla, a soul incarnated on this prison planet that was experiencing its second reincarnation. This helped him to be more perceptible to the *Shock Wave of Awareness* and endowed him with great intelligence. His great creativity led him to become one of the best inventors in history, with thousands of patents under his name that helped him to completely change the life of humankind, such as for example the discovery of the alternating current that we use in our daily life.

In addition, he invented a type of radio device that could pick up signals of the Moon emitted by the Pleiadeans that controlled it, and in a short time, he managed to decode them to start receiving messages from them.

The Pleiadeans took advantage of this conversation with Tesla to provide him with a lot of knowledge that would help to improve the living conditions of humankind through technology. This helped Nikola to create plenty of very advanced devices for his time. For example, x-rays or electrical transmission without wires.

However, despite being a very bright mind, the ruling elite of the time was always in opposition to him; and he always was in a bad economic situation. Thomas Edison, for example, had him working for several years, stealing several patents and inventions that were not his. Their rivalry reached a peak in the famous *War of the Currents*, in which Edison supported the Continuous Current and Tesla the Alternating Current, winning the alternating current because it was more effective and more economical. Since then, Edison, characterized by a big ego, always tried to humiliate him and crush him with all the power available at the time.

Due to the lack of money, Tesla did not have another choice but to create weapons for the army, as the famous *Death Ray*, a lethal weapon that was capable of firing a ray at a great distance, destroying everything in its path. Fortunately, the Pleiadeans advised him that he should deliver that weapon, but with a failure so that it was not used. So he did. And in the demonstration, it was a great success, and he received the agreed payment, however, at the time of delivery, this did not work. This caused the rivalry with the government of the U. S., which from that moment began to constantly monitor him.

Tesla had a dream: to be able to transmit energy for free to all over the world without wires through a tower that was emitting electromagnetic waves. And he almost achieved it, with the famous Wardenclyffe Tower project, funded by the banker J.P. Morgan, a member of the Illuminati of Bavaria.

Although, all these great inventions on Earth did not arouse the minimum interest in the Anunnaki, because each one was concerned to implement their own agenda.

When Anu realized that Tesla could provide the world with energy for free, he quickly instructed his Illuminati subjects to stop this, because his plan was that humans devastated the Earth's natural resources up to the point at which the planet reduced the population itself, up to the point of putting an end to its own illness, that is to say, us, because if Anu could not convince humans to destroy each other through free will to keep us under control, they could slip out of his manipulation. So he devised a plan B for the destruction of the planet so the Earth reduced the population in the near future. Such a master plan…

J.P. Morgan, following the orders of the Illuminati of

Bavaria, decided to cancel the construction of the tower, leaving unfinished, and the dream of Tesla, under the pretext that this project was not going to give him any economic benefit.

Tesla tried to convince him that he could charge a modest amount of energy to consumers if he wished so, but to let him finish. Morgan, obviously, was not convinced and left unfinished the work that would have changed the history of humankind completely.

The elite of those times, infiltrated by the Illuminati of Bavaria, made sure to erase the name of Nikola Tesla from the history. They even took credit for the invention of the radio and gave it to Marconi, even when after his death, in the 1960s, Supreme Court of the United States dictated that the patent on the radio was rightfully the property of Tesla, legally recognizing him as the inventor of this. Although, this was hidden by the Elite so that the world did not know it.

Tesla died on January 7, 1943, in poverty and absolute solitude, and since then, the US government took the patents of this huge genius.

In the face of all these scientific and technological advances of humankind, it was obvious that the negative energy received from the humans had decreased considerably. The Draconians did not like this, and they sent a contingent to visit the Usumgal Anunnaki to demand them to increase the negative energies from their farm or their agreement would come to an end.

At this threat, Anu decided to abide by the order and explained that the drop in energy harvesting, was due to a clash of a wave of awareness coming from the fifth dimension, however, it was already over. They had been free to increase the chaos on Earth, and therefore, the negative energy of the Lulus. He predicted a significant increase in the coming years on Earth, and he was quite right!

Like Nikola Tesla, at the end of the Clash of the Wave of Awareness, it was born another embodied soul, more exactly, in its third incarnation on Earth. This soul would acquire the gift of Oratory, and this would change the history. His name was Adolf Hitler...

Hitler

While Tesla registered hundreds of patents, Enlil uses an opportunity to communicate with a British man who could use the phase, his name, Aleister Crowley, born on October 12, 1875, and heir to a large fortune after the death of his father.

Aleister represented a great opportunity for Enlil to create various secret societies that followed his occult teachings, and thus, not to depend on his Chosen People to impose his plans. In addition, for a long time, he had been wanting to create hidden societies to match his father, Anu.

Crowley fulfilled its role magnificently because his devotion to the occult teachings led him to fanaticism. Enlil introduced himself to Crowley with the name of Aiwass or Baphomet, since he did not want to be associated with Yahweh or with his Anunnaki past. Aleister Crowley initially tried to take control of a secret society called the *Hermetic Order of the Golden Dawn*, the famous Golden Dawn, which followed the teachings of the White Brotherhoods. However, when he could not impose his ideas, he left the Order and created his own occultist society, Astrum Argentum, also reaching to the level of being the visible head of other secret societies such as the *OTO*, Ordo Templi Orientis, among others.

Enlil manipulated Crowley teaching him diverse knowledge of magic under the maximum premise of overcoming materialism and food of the ego, with pleasant sensations in the body without the intervention of feelings and destroying the spirit.

Aleister created a series of laws called *Thelema*, and also wrote a book called *The Book of the Law*, which was based on a single premise: "Do what thou wilt".

Modern Satanism was born. The success of Crowley was such that even following the instructions of his manipulator, Enlil, he attempted to open a portal in the United States for which the Anunnaki could communicate with the entire population without the need for the phase. Fortunately, he failed.

Enlil realized that what had been achieved by Crowley not only had to stay among the followers of his doctrine in the secret societies, but it had to replicate on the entire population, since, if he could make people simply concerned about feeding their banal desires, this would destroy their spirit and their connection with the Source of Origin. So he began to devise a plan to achieve this so that people would accept it little by little without realizing it.

Enki, realizing that Nikola Tesla was being boycotted by the global elite, tried to use to a German with the ability to convince, with which, he had managed to contact through the phase fortuitously, because this man had the ability to enter the phase unconsciously, his name, Adolf Hitler, a soul incarnated on Earth suffering its third incarnation. He was born on April 20, 1889, and since very child, he was severely beaten by his father, Alois. This was critical to mark the cold and isolated personality that would mark the whole life of Adolf.

Enki established his first communication with Adolf, and it was accidentally since Enki was trying to communicate with a member of the White Brotherhood. However, he realized that Hitler could hear him. Out of curiosity, Enki observed the young Adolf Hitler had dropped out of school and was engaged in painting pictures. Just when Enki was losing interest in him, Hitler was giving a speech in the public square where he spoke of a hidden power that handled the governments like puppets. But this was not what drew the most attention to Enki, but to see his little audience listening attentively as if they were hypnotized. At that moment, Enki realized that Hitler was the person he was looking for. His plan was to take advantage of the endowments of conviction that he had to awaken people, and finally get rid of the control and manipulation of the government in the shadows that controlled Anu and Enlil. His first step was inviting him to his secret society of Thule, which took him one Earth year to convince him. There, Enki realized the harsh personality of Hitler.

Once entering this secret society, controlled by Enki, Hitler began to receive hidden knowledge that would help him improve his gift of Oratory and conviction of the masses; in addition, it was revealed to him that the world was ruled from the shadows by Zionism, the Chosen People of Enlil. This aroused in Hitler a deep *anti-Semitic* feeling. Although Enki had no doubt of the oratory features of Hitler, he had doubts with regards to his cold personality, he saw psychopathic traits in him. Although for the liberation of humankind, it was worth the risk.

While Hitler was being trained, Anu, pressured by the Draconians, began to move all the secret societies under his command, to start a war on a global scale never seen before.

And that is how on July 28, 1914, the First World War began, which took the lives of more than nine million people. Something that triggered the increased uptake of the negative energy of the human farm in the history of the Earth, not only because of the conflict itself, and the deaths but also of the fear the world lived in thanks to the press that gave details of this Great War. The Draconians were happy.

With this war, Anu showed the power of having secret societies under his control, as he had managed them in such secret, that neither Enki nor Enlil could realize it.

At this dark world panorama, Enki began to move the White Brotherhoods that he still controlled, without the influence of the Jesuits, and let this conflict last only four years. In addition to the opportunity to put Hitler on the world scene, since he knew that with his speeches and oratory he was not going to get far. He had to empower him. That is to say, give Hitler power so his speeches would liberate all humankind. So, he convinced Hitler to enroll in the army, since that was the only way to rise to power. As with unfinished studies and on a low income, he could not think of another way.

At the end of the First World War, it began Hitler's meteoric rise to power, which put in check the plans of Enlil and Anu, since he was about to put an end to the international Zionism.

But why he did not get it? What was the error of Hitler? How did he get so quickly to power? To whom did the Second World War benefit? For whom did Hitler really worked...?

The Consequences of a Bad Choice

At the end of the First World War, Hitler had not made much progress in his military career, so Enki began to connect him with various members of secret societies who were occupying strategic positions in the German government. And thanks to the great power of conviction of Hitler, he quickly started gaining friends who provided his rise to power.

As well as Hitler increased the number of friends in positions of power, it also increased his ego, because he felt he was a sort of chosen one who could talk to God. Because he believed that the communication he had with Enki, in reality, was with God himself. This increased his self-confidence and thirst for power to the point of, in the year 1923, he had already related and fully into the German politics, and counting with a large number of friends who supported him, attempted a very improvised coup d'état, which was called the Munich, but it failed, and he was sentenced to five years in prison.

This concerned Enki, because he realized that the psychopathy and thirst for power of Hitler were growing more and more. So, during his time in prison, Enki tried to convince him that his mission was to liberate humankind and not only to obtain power, and apparently, he did so, but not for long.

Upon his releasing, Germany was undergoing an

important economic and social crisis. There was much violence in the streets and people had the feeling that the government was incapable of ruling, which led to a power absence and general discontent. This opened the doors for Hitler and his National Socialist Party to rise to power in 1933 as the last and only salvation for the German, as these were worried about the loss of their material goods and their work opportunities.

Although, it should be noted that all this atmosphere of chaos in Germany was caused precisely by the members of the White Dragon, all with the aim of giving a chance to Hitler. The early years of government of the Fuehrer were very prosperous for Germany. The job offer increased considerably and the economy was growing. The crisis was over.

The Fuehrer used the secret symbolism that he learned at the secret society of Thule to hypnotize the masses, taking up the symbol of the black sun as the logo of his political party. His fanaticism for the occultism was such that he even started a campaign to search for objects of power as the Ark of the Covenant or the Lance of Longinus since he believed that having them, his power would be such that he could become immortal.

Enki, seeing the speeches that hypnotized thousands of Germans, was convinced that Hitler was the right person. His plan was to liberate the German first, and then. All the other countries. Even though he did not know how to do it.

While all this was happening in Germany, Enlil was working on a secret plan to zombify the whole world and began to contact several scientists, members of the secret lodges, to create a device capable of transmitting images to all over the world. It took a long time, until finally, Philo T. Farnsworth, an American follower of the Church of Jesus Christ of Latter-day Saints, created by Enlil, succeeded in creating the first electronic image dissector in 1927, which, afterward would be refined and known as the television. One of the most prolific inventions to achieve control of humankind.

Upon finding this out, Enki saw a great opportunity to convey the messages of the Fuehrer to all over the world and, thus, achieve waking them up. Hitler had not called the attention of Anu and Enlil until the Fuehrer decided to ban the banks belonging to the Rothschild in Germany. This quickly sounded the alarms of Anu and Enlil, who realized of everything he was doing in Germany and discovered that Enki was behind this.

Enlil proposed Anu to end up Hitler as he represented a major threat to their plans. However, Anu marveled at the oratory and conviction skills that the Fuehrer had, he decided to establish contact with him to convince him of everything contrary to what Enki had taught him. This was not very difficult, as Hitler, entering the phase unconsciously, could establish contact with any Anunnaki who wanted to.

Anu began to manipulate Hitler, telling him that the only way to defeat Zionism was to destroy it throughout the world, taking advantage of the big ego and thirst for power of Hitler, it was not very difficult to convince him. And, in order Enki did not suspect anything, he instructed Enlil to pretend a few failed attacks against

Hitler so that Enki thought that they were trying to assassinate him to remove the Illuminati banks from Germany.

This misled Enki, who did not notice this secret plan of Anu, although he realized that Hitler was investing a large part of the taxes to increase his army. Hitler confused by the voices that he listened when he entered the phase, was convinced that the Holy Trinity was talking to him and that he was protected by God because all the attacks against him always failed. Although his army and weapons had increased significantly, they were not enough to achieve the goal of creating a huge empire and destroy Zionism altogether. So, Anu advised him to get the support of Prescott Bush, a man of Wall Street that served as the nominee of the Illuminati, for Hitler not to suspect it, who could sell him the weapons and oil required to carry out his plan.

This was the big mistake of Hitler, having accepted the foreign funding to carry out his plans, as in doing so, he became immediately in their slave.

Anu had planned everything to create a great conflict at a global level, with which the negative energies captured would increase again. And that was how on September 1, 1939, the Second World War started with the German invasion of Poland.

Since the end of 1939 until the beginning of 1941, Germany produced a series of dazzling military campaigns and treaties, with which he conquered and subdued much of continental Europe. During the Second World War, the German army massacred more than 100,000 Jews and more than 10,000 gypsies. And conducted several experiments with them. Although after this war, the winners inflated these figures in the history books.

Germany had already conquered much of Europe. However, Bush prohibited Hitler to attack Switzerland, central of the Rothschild Illuminati banks, because if he did it, weapons and oil would end. Then, the German army crossed Switzerland without touching anything. Switzerland, without an army, was easy to conquer, but he did not do so out of fear that his funding ended.

In this second Great War at a global level, Anu not only was as a spectator but he also mobilized the grey ones into their flying saucers to achieve victories that he saw convenient. That is to say, he left nothing to chance. He was also anxious for the United States to enter the war, and thus, be able to test a weapon the Illuminati were financing. So he convinced his subjects infiltrated in the U.S. government to let Japan attack them so that they had the perfect pretext to enter into this war. Japan fell into the trap and attacked Pearl Harbor without any resistance in 1941, and the United States entered the world war.

With this Great War, the Draconians were ecstatic, because, with this great World War II, the Usumgal Anunnaki had tripled the energy captured from their human farm.

Enki was disappointed and felt responsible for the behavior of Hitler and the great world war that he had caused. He was increasingly losing hope in human beings. Although, he later realized that Anu was behind all this.

The Great War ended in 1945 with the alleged suicide of Hitler and the explosion of the atomic bombs in Hiroshima and Nagasaki.

In reality, the Fuehrer, made a deal with the allies to let him live and escape to Argentina where he lived for many years, in exchange for his most prominent scientists and technologies were donated to the victorious power nations of war. This was how the dream of Enki to liberate humankind came to an end.

The explosion of nuclear bombs alerted the Intraterrestrials who went to the Galactic Confederation to explain the situation and ask permission to attack human beings, because, in their view, these jeopardized the integrity of planet Uras, Earth...

The Great Lie of the Arrival to the Moon

At the end of the Second World War, the United Nations (UN) was founded. In 1945, representatives of 50 countries met in San Francisco to write the Charter of the United Nations. Obviously, this new organization was full of Zionist leaders and Illuminati, which opened the door for the Zionism to claim the state of Israel as their Promised Land, since, in 1948, the UN assigned the State of Israel to the Zionists.

Finally, the Zionism had a territory of its own and was at the top of the world power. The promise of their God Yahweh, Enlil, made thousands of years ago, had been fulfilled.

The Intraterrestrials, who were in the Abzu of the Earth, decided to file a complaint to the Galactic Confederation through the Carians, because for them the Second World War, provoked by humans, and the use of atomic bombs, jeopardized the health of the planet Uras, Earth, and they requested permission to intervene against human beings.

The Galactic Confederation decided to give humans another opportunity, because, for them, the atomic bomb was not as powerful to put on risk the planet Earth, their prison planet. But they did approve the Carians and Intraterrestrials to tell the world leaders that in case of another war, on a global scale, with atomic weapons, they would get involved. And so it was that in the year 1947, in a secret meeting with world leaders at the time, the Carians and Intraterrestrials warned them about the risk of having another confrontation on a large scale using mass destruction weapons.

This was a radical change in human history, which opened the doors to other extraterrestrial races to get in contact with the human race for their own interests. For example, the grey ones, who wanted to get rid of the Reptilians, made a secret pact with the US government when, in 1947, a ship of the grey ones crashed in Roswell and was captured by the Government of the United States. Since then, the grey ones made a deal with them to allow them to carry out abductions of people to conduct different genetic experiments for the creation of hybrids that could live infiltrated into humankind and, thus, get rid of the reptilian control. All in exchange for alien technology to give them an advantage over the other countries.

On the one hand, the Insectoids sent a contingent to the Earth and made contact with the leaders of the Soviet Union and made a deal with them for the extraction of natural resources in exchange of alien technology.

With these deals, the grey ones and the Insectoids made sure not to violate the law of free will. Since then, up to now, the Exopolitics *(hypothetical political relations between aliens and humans)*, has marked the history of humankind.

With the progress achieved by the Soviet Union and the United States, they started an arms race to see which was the world superpower. Which developed into the famous *Cold War*, which was a political, economic, military, and scientific confrontation between the Western capitalist bloc, led by the United States, and the Eastern Communist Party, led by the Soviet Union.

It is known as the Cold War since none of the two blocks ever took direct action against the other. The Anunnaki took advantage of this and continued making human sacrifices for the recollection of negative energies and thus, they created conflicts, such as *the Greek Civil War, the Korean War, the Vietnam War, The First War in Afghanistan, the Civil War in Lebanon, the war in Angola, the Indo-Pakistani War, The Gulf War, etc.*, and therefore, continued to feed the Draconians in a more discreet and subtle way.

While this conflict was carried out, and humankind was in constant fear, the television began to become popular throughout the world. And soon, the Dark Elite, advised by Enlil, realized that it was an artifact with which they could manipulate the opinion and thoughts of people. In other words, the Elite began to use television to zombify humankind.

The United States and the Soviet Union were also engaged in a Space Race, which began with the launch of the Sputnik 1 in 1957, the first human artifact capable of reaching space and orbiting the planet itself. The first milestone in the space race was achieved by the Soviets since in the same year, they launched the Sputnik 2. And inside the ship, the first living being came out into space: a Kudriavka dog, named Layka, who died seven hours after getting out of the atmosphere.

The next milestone was also achieved by the Soviets

[margin note, left: FALSE HISTORY USA DID GO TO MOON]

by launching in 1961 the Vostok 1, manned by Yuri Gagarin, the first human being to go to space and return safe and sound.

In the face of such disadvantage, and to justify the waste of taxes in the creation of NASA, <u>the US government decided to deceive the whole world with a false arrival to the Moon to gain an advantage against the Soviet Union</u>. And for this, they would use <u>television</u>, the new invention to manipulate society as a whole. [handwritten: USA DID GO TO MOON]

So, they decided to hire Stanley Kubrick to film this show in a Hollywood studio, with which, they were able to deceive the whole world. Obviously with the support of the Illuminati, who were interested in implementing capitalism throughout the world so as to continue increasing their economic power.

It is no surprise that the craft that reached the moon had the name of Apollo <u>"11"</u>, a <u>Kabbalistic number</u> of the Illuminati.

Although it should be noted that Kubrick regretted of this great deception and left us many messages in his films for us to decipher (like the movie that was based on the book *"The Shining"*, written by the brilliant writer Stephen King), which it cost him his life.

This American victory, with the false arrival to the Moon, was the beginning of the decline of the Soviet Union. But, how it was that this superpower lost the Cold War and dissolved so fast? What was the covenant they made...?

[handwritten footer: ★ REVISIONISM BULLSHIT IN THIS BOOK! NO DISCUSSION OF NAZI RELATIONSHIP ¢ REPTILIANS & THEIR AID IN DEVELOPING ROCKETS & TIME MACHINE DIE GLOCKE]

The Destiny of the Human Farm

After the tremendous blow and the destruction of the dream of implanting the communism throughout the world of the Soviet Union, this was only an experiment conducted by the Illuminati to measure the power of manipulation that the television had in those moments.

This device was able to convince all people of what they wanted. Basically, the television could rewrite history to suit themselves. Since then, the elite began to invest large amounts of money in the world of entertainment, both in television, like cinema and music, etc.

Enlil, seeing the power of influence in humans of television, decided that his Chosen People would become the administrators of the world entertainment, giving them all the television companies and Hollywood, with which he would manipulate the thoughts of humankind. While Anu gave the control of the world economy to the Illuminati and to the Jesuits the control of churches and religions in the world.

With this Enlil and Anu made sure of having control over the minds of humankind and their farm was taking shape little by little. They did not want to make the same error of the past, in which humans rebelled to their submission, and decided that the human Lulus would not have time to think and to liberate themselves, even they would not realize that they were living as slaves in an artificial matrix created by them.

To achieve this, they entrusted the Government of the United States to invest in different secret programs as the MK-ULTRA and Monarch Project to study the human mind and understand it without the population noticing it.

In addition, Enlil commissioned the Zionists, His Chosen People, to do the same, but through the entertainment industry, so they decided to create a database at the Tavistock Institute from which they would create the trends and the unique thought of the masses to manipulate them as if they were puppets. An example of that was the hippie movement of the 60s & 70s, at which they led teenagers to try synthetic drugs and to try drugs without love under the false belief that they were the resistance and the group of protest at that time.

During this time, the human sacrifices in the form of wars did not cease. A clear example was the Vietnam War which killed more than a million people. The Reptilians were pleased by the energy captured from Uras, Earth. However, fearful that Jesus sent a wave of energy of awareness to the Earth, they instructed the Anunnaki to accelerate the extraction of the blood of the Earth, which is the oil, to lower its vibrational frequency and thus, mitigate the reception of waves of awareness by the planet.

That is why Anu used his secret society, the Illuminati, to create oil companies and stay with the control of the energy of the planet. And by the way, weaken it a little. Since then, no alternative energy is allowed all over the world.

The Pleiadeans, who were in the Moon, seeing that several extraterrestrial races were already interacting with the Earth, decided to intervene in a discreet manner to help the awakening of humankind. So they started to contact several humans by conveying different knowledge and tips to save the human race. These contacts managed to convey the message and to make a little balance.

While all of this was happening, the humans who were on Mars and that lived with the Intraterrestrials and Carians managed to achieve a significant breakthrough in their evolution. To the level of practicing telekinesis and telepathy.

The Galactic Confederation, seeing this great step in so little time, decided to send several spy emissaries to monitor closely these humans, since they were afraid that another Jesus appeared.

Enki, seeing that humankind on Earth was being manipulated and totally controlled, and that they showed no signs of evolution, decided to wait and counteract the blows of his brother Enlil and his father Anu through his secret lodge of the White Dragons, since upon the intervention of so many extraterrestrial races on Earth, it was inevitable that human technology would advance, and his arrival in the digital era was inevitable. So, he decided that to happen in order to use that technology to help humankind. In addition, he wanted to wait for the second wave of awareness that Jesus had promised so the liberation of the Lulus would be easier.

In the year 1989 in the Earth, the grey ones were still doing experiments to successfully mix human DNA with theirs for the creation of a hybrid that would live free, infiltrated among humans. They had not yet achieved it.

The computers and chips were increasingly up-to-date, and as Enki predicted, humankind was venturing into the *Digital Age*.

The Soviet Union, worn out by all natural resources that they yielded to the Insectoids in exchange for technology, decided to make a peace treaty with the United States to let them win the Cold War, while they recovered and continued understanding and using the technology of these Insectoids beings.

And on November 9, 1989, the Berlin Wall fell, and with it, the triumph of capitalism in the world was confirmed. This opened the doors for the Illuminati to fully implement their *New World Order*, with which they would have total control of Humankind...

The Beginning of the New World Order

Coming to an agreement between the United States and the Soviet Union, to implant in the world the capitalism, it became clear that the law of the jungle was applied to the World Economy.

With this, the Illuminati finally moved towards globalization. And they gained ground to implant their long-awaited New World Order that they were looking for many decades ago, and that they had not been able to make thanks to the halt imposed by the members of the Brotherhood of the White Dragon.

Enki had learned that, to stop the progress of Anu and Enlil, he not only had to return to the Brotherhood of the White Dragon, but also had to infiltrate its members in key positions of power in order to curb the dark plans of the Illuminati, which up to that time, he had achieved it. However, Anu and Enlil, with the help of television, they knew they could introduce the New World Order in the collective unconscious and thus, create a reality at their whim.

Previously, they promoted it with books such as George Orwell's *1984*, or *A Happy World* by Aldous Huxley. Or through comics and science fiction stories in Hollywood. But they realized that these media did not reach many people, but only a few. And in this way, they had failed to implement the idea in the collective unconscious of the majority and therefore, their goal had failed to materialize. But now, with the success of the television, they could easily deploy their idea through subliminal and hidden messages and, in this way, introduce the idea in a large number of people without them noticing it.

So they did not take long to proclaim it to the whole world. And in January of 1991, shortly after the Gulf war, they used a puppet controlled by Illuminati named George Bush (father), who was president of the United States at that time, and took advantage of a speech he gave at the national chain in which he announced the beginning of the New World Order. Anu and Enlil calculated that this would be implemented in seven or nine years approximately. However, the actions of the White Dragon did not allow it. Or at least, not at all.

Covert wars or sacrifices continued throughout the world, and the human farm was feeding the Draconians and Anunnaki Reptilians.

By 1997 the Insectoids had already finished removing the natural resources they needed for their planet. They had a covenant of peace with the Reptilians after the Great Galactic War in which they participated. However, they put at risk this peace treaty. Far from leaving Uras, Earth, they only pretended to go so the Anunnaki did not suspect it, since they left several of their species infiltrated and hidden among the humans of Russia, and continued to exchange knowledge and technology with them so they could compete in the future, to be the first world power and thus, be able to wrest control of the human farm to the Usumgal Anunnaki.

The Illuminati, desperate because they could not realize their new world order, were preparing a big blow to create a Third World War that would guarantee the total control of the world. Advised by Anu in the year 2001, they decided to attack the most significant symbol of the world economy: the World Trade Center, disguised as a false flag. They predicted that this blow would be sufficient to unleash the chaos required to create a new war on a world scale. But it was not so, because the White Dragon acted fast and did not allow most of the nations to take actions because of this attack. In addition, the Insectoids advised Russia not to take sides, because they were sure it was a ploy of the Usumgal Anunnaki.

Despite the fact that this attack generated a wave of fear throughout the world, and substantially increased the negative energy captured by the Draconians, Enlil and Anu were really surprised that humankind was getting tired of wars, but they did not give up. To Enlil, it occurred that the new sacrifices, in addition, to disguise them as wars, they would also be disguised as terrorism and instructed his Chosen People to finance more attacks around the world.

September 11 was not only a date that changed history and that implanted fear in the world, but it was also used as an experiment to see if the collective unconscious helped create the reality much quicker, as this event had been encrypted previously announced in several movies, series, and cartoons; and they succeeded in doing so. With this, the Illuminati were able to measure the effectiveness of the hidden messages for implantation in the collective subconscious in order to, later become a reality. Since then, the media bombardment of this type of message is constantly increasing, since they knew very well that the collective thinking can change reality at its whim.

At the beginning of 2000, new technologies flooded the world. And one, in particular, promoted by the White Dragon, became the hope of Enki to help the awakening of humankind occur once and for all. This technology was the Internet. With it, Enki thought to counter the television and begin to transmit messages contrary to it for the awakening of human consciousness. Although refine it and making it popular in the world took several years.

Little by little, this became the only channel to talk about what was going on in the world. It was thanks to the internet that people knew of the secret lodges that govern the world behind the scenes and their dark plans to introduce the New World Order. In short, it began the slow awakening of humankind.

When Enlil and Anu realized that the Internet was contrary to their plans, they began to try to control it. They knew they had little time to carry out their plans since the Second Wave of Awareness, prepared by Jesus from the fifth dimension, was about to come to Earth and they were afraid that their plans would not be finished by then. So, they began to use the Chosen People, the Illuminati and all their secret lodges to accelerate their objective and once and for all establish their New World Order…

We Are the Ultimate Light

Enki put all his hopes on the Internet for the awakening of the consciousness of the people. This technology became the only mass media which was not controlled by the Illuminati and which exposed the true origin of the human being, and in addition, it revealed who the real enemies of humankind were.

The Brotherhood of the White Dragon did a magnificent job to disseminate these ideas through this medium which slowly began to grow. This bothered Enlil because, for the first time, the best-kept secrets of the Anunnaki were finally revealed to humankind. He knew that the potential of this technology was immense. What bothered him was that there was nothing he could do, since the Internet was totally controlled by the members of the White Dragon. So, he took the only weak point that the Internet had: its openness and total freedom. He immediately instructed his Chosen People to begin to invest in this new technology and to flood it with contents that would control the masses. As he had done with the television.

If he could not control the Internet, at least he was going to take advantage of it and flood it with spam to confuse people more. And that was how the famous social networks were born, with which they wanted to control the masses.

The success of the networks was immediate, as these

social networks were used to extract the information from all users: their names, their address, their likings, their friends, their relatives, etc., and facilitated the search of any person. It marked the beginning of the total control of users. Finally, the much awaited *Orwellian World* became reality. Although there was one more step to get this technology to have the impact they wanted.

Enlil was convinced that the human Lulus were a race much lower, self-destructive by nature and that they did not have the slightest hope to evolve on this planet prison. So he asked Anu the hidden technology with which they could zombify the whole humankind once and for all, but he refused, because contrary to what Enlil thought, Anu believed that the Lulus had great potential and he feared that they would evolve to the extent that Jesus did. So, these technologies that his Anunnaki subjects had developed, remained still hidden. However, at the insistence of Enlil, he was convinced and decided to release this technology with which humans could have internet all the time in the palm of their hands. Thus, there were born the Wi-Fi and Smartphones, which were able to connect to the Internet at all times.

Enlil knew that this represented a great opportunity for the world to use social networks and be connected, such as a hive mind, with ideas that they wanted to impose on us.

Enki, surprised by the release of this technology, saw in it a great opportunity to continue awakening human minds, and even more when the wave of awareness that

Jesus was going to send to Earth was close. Enki firmly believed that this was a big mistake of his father Anu and that it would mean the liberation of humankind.

Anu, fearful that with this technology he started to awaken humans, instructed his Illuminati subjects to, little by little, legislate laws that took control of the internet, as he already had done with other media.

It was 2007, and Jesus was almost ready to send the second wave of awareness to the Earth, so he contacted the Pleiadeans to calibrated and prepare the Moon. Jesus told them that he wanted to take advantage of the winter solstice to maximize the impact of the shock and to last as long as possible.

The Pleiadeans got to work and calculated that the Moon would be ready within five Earth years approximately.

When Anu and Enlil found out the date on which the wave of awareness would collide with the Earth, they began to try to revert it. So they came up with the idea of spreading the false Maya prophecy of the end of the world in all its media and across the internet, and also instructed to make a catastrophe film so in the subconscious of people, it converted this date of the awakening of consciousness, in a catastrophic and terrific date. With this, he wanted to minimize the impact of this Wave of awareness sent by Jesus.

Enki was frustrated because, despite the fact that many people were waking up thanks to the internet, the vast majority had fallen into the trap of Enlil. And they only used social networks and trivial content. And for the hundredth time, he lost faith in humankind and began to think if Enlil was right and humans were a race doomed not to evolve. His last hope was the next wave of awareness, so he instructed the members of the White Dragon to use social networks and disseminate the Anunnaki secrets. In addition to deny the prophecy of the end of the world about which humankind was worried.

The day finally came. On December 21, 2012, the second wave of awareness came to Earth and would have an approximate duration of 13 years.

Since then, humankind is increasingly concerned about their environment, they feel more empathy towards animals, and they believe less and less in the rotten system in which they live. The awakening of humankind had begun. But not at the pace that Enki and Jesus himself would like since the awakening has been slow. This is due to the Illuminati plan to normalize their bizarre rituals, because, after that day, they have been responsible for bombing the population with dark messages through all their media, and are trying to normalize all their aberrations.

Enlil was frustrated with this new wave of awareness, as his new order had not been completed. However, he did not quit and entrusted his Chosen People to continue with their agenda.

Enki with this plan of conscience, slow, but assertive, regained faith in humankind and continued leading the Brotherhood of the White Dragon to hinder all the plans of his father and brother.

While this was happening, the grey ones had already managed to infiltrate between humans their new hybrid race, half human - half grey ones, with which they ensured the continuity of their kind and prepared in secret to rebel against the Draconians.

The Kadistu had a meeting with the leaders of the Galactic Confederation by 2013, and among other issues, they addressed the Wave of Awareness that Jesus once more had sent to Earth, and decided to give humans the last opportunity and not to intervene, since they were afraid that another human could reach the level of Jesus, they also knew that the human race was one of the few with the gift of expressing feelings. So, it was worth taking the risk this race would evolve by itself. With the Galactic Confederation, they agreed that this would be the last wave of Awareness that humans would have since when it ended, the Kadistu would join together to lock the power of Jesus and not allow him to help again. Because they knew that if the humans of Earth did not evolve, they would focus on the advanced humans who were on Mars, and would leave Uras, Earth, as one of the prison planets more difficult to overcome.

In the year 2015, an unexpected galactic event happened. The extraterrestrial race of Felines decided to declare war on the Draconians for an alleged invasion that they had made to a planet controlled by the Felines. This put on red alert to the Galactic Confederation and the whole galaxy, since the Felines were the only race able to beat the Reptilians.

With this event, the Draconians that took care of the farm and gave orders to Anu and the Usumgal Anunnaki had to withdraw to join the war against the

Felines. Anu saw a magnificent opportunity to finally get rid of the Draconians control, since he had realized that, for more than half of his life, he had been enslaved by them and the Lulus. He said to Enlil, Enki, and his entire fleet to escape to a planet away from the war. Everyone accepted, but Enlil and Enki, since they wanted to finish what they had begun. And at that moment, he realized that his two sons were obsessed with the human race and there was nothing he could do.

Anu and his fleet escaped from the astral bottom of the fourth dimension and decided to materialize in the third dimension. In a lonely planet away from the war that their race was carrying out. Anu knew that there, on that planet, he wanted to live the last years of his life.

With the fleeing of Anu, the balance of forces arrived to achieve their mission.

The Insectoids, for their part, had their own agenda to seize control of the farm. So they prepared Russia to become the new empire when deploying their new order.

However, Enlil is moving his Chosen People and the Illuminati to prevent it and continue with control of the Earth.

The Intraterrestrials started to monitor the Insectoids to prevent their plan to succeed.

The Carians were more interested in trying to end the war between The Draconians and the Felines than in the Earth.

Enki knew that with the withdrawal of the Draconians and the momentary withdrawal of Anu, this was a unique opportunity for humankind to be liberated.

But this does not depend on Jesus, nor Enki, nor any other extraterrestrial race that wanted to help us. The awakening depends on ourselves. We are at a point where the New Order is close to being implanted, but also close to humankind fully awake. It is up to us the end that we want to give this story.

It is time to wake up!

NOTE

Dear reader, I know that everything you just read is a little science fiction story. But there is something certain in all this.

You must continue to love your religion above all else. It does not matter that. It is better to continue living the normal life you currently have. But I know that some of my readers will think the same as me.

Those are the ones who started waking up.

ANUNNAKI

Reptilians beyond Myth, Science And Humankind

by

Henry Krane

The majestic kingdom of Akkad, the forgotten region of Sumer, many of its stories were lost in the sands of time. The Anunnaki are only almost a forgotten memory in the mountains of the origin of creation. But what do we know about the first gods of humankind? This book is an investigation that will provide the readers with unknown data that they will not find anywhere else. I put my reputation to the test in this book. This book is based on the writings and translations of the few scholars who understand and can translate the content of the Sumerian tablets. The Anunnaki gods lived and had many stories. These are their secrets...

Introduction

The Anunnaki, those gods who created us or that we heard many researchers talk about more than twenty years ago, these researchers told us that they were gods from the stars who came to create us through genetic manipulation of the DNA of a hominid or primate, which they made evolve into a homo sapiens by adding their DNA into the DNA of that monkey.

The Anunnaki, those beings who came from the planet Nibiru to make us evolve, enslaved us by making us work inside gold mines.

That is what those researchers tell us happened, but that is false. There is a very distinct history of the Anunnaki according to these scholars who can understand, translate, and read the Sumerian tablets.

80% of the tablets were destroyed, so some parts could not be translated and read by these scholars. Zecharia Sitchin decided to ignore this and created a story about the Anunnaki as we know it today. Besides that, he invented dialogues.

What you will find in this book is reliable knowledge from these scholars as most of them do not lie when they state that they cannot read part of these tablets, because they are destroyed and in bad condition. So that can be called humility and objectivity to understand the Anunnaki story much better.

Zecharia Sitchin was the first to make this truth public; because of him, the world knew about the existence of this extraterrestrial race. It was a positive thing that Zecharia Sitchin made humankind awaken and motivated it to investigate the Anunnaki, but obviously, everything he says is inventions, science fiction stories that do not show us the truth behind the myth.

How do we know that? In his books, there are long dialogues between Anunnaki, dialogues of people who spoke with the gods, dialogues so extensive, nonexistent in the Sumerian tablets. All this is irrefutable proof that Zecharia Sitchin lied. Those dialogues do not exist on tablets.

Then there is another piece of proof: the gold that was collected to repair the atmosphere of the hypothetical planet Nibiru. This planet does not exist nor is it mentioned in the Sumerian tablets.

In addition, there are some events that Sitchin does not mention but that exist in the Sumerian tablets, for example, the planet Tiamat.

With this, it is demonstrated that what Zecharia Sitchin said is an interpretation of his, which is respectable but it is a false story.

His books are not based 100% on what the remains of the Sumerian tablets say. So everything he wrote is simply made-up stories.

I will prove it to you.

Akkad and Sumer

Let's start with the ancient and mysterious Sumerian civilization. This civilization reached its peak more than 3500 years before Christ. However, there was a small population that preceded the Sumerians, dating back to 5800 years BC. The time gap between these two populations is truly enormous.

After some time, Sumer began to decline and was assimilated by the Akkadians. The Akkadians adopted all the customs, gods, and mythology of the Sumerians. They copied the entirety of Sumerian knowledge and culture, adapting it to their own interests. The Sumerians used cuneiform texts and writings, inscribed on clay tablets that contained the history of the ancient Sumerians.

However, it is not widely discussed that the Sumerians left behind more than just clay tablets. The entire history of the Sumerians was also documented on large stone cylinders or scrolls, which depicted scenes from the mythology of the gods and various rituals. Unfortunately, many researchers have overlooked these stone cylinders.

Another noteworthy point is that when the Akkadians absorbed and conquered the Sumerians, they made changes to the Sumerian writing system. The Sumerian script was complex, so the Akkadians simplified it. As a result, the Akkadian and Sumerian scripts bear a striking resemblance to each other.

A curious fact is that to this day, the origin of Sumerian writing remains unknown. The immense complexity of Sumerian writing and its unexpected emergence in a small town known as Obeid or Ubaid (which dates back 5800 years before Christ) make it challenging to determine the origin of Sumerian civilization. It remains a mystery that has yet to be solved. However, as mentioned earlier, the Akkadians had to develop a much simpler writing system to accommodate their language.

Another intriguing fact is that not all Sumerian tablets are accessible to the public. Many have disappeared, others have been destroyed, and there are those awaiting study in museum warehouses. It is true that numerous museums around the world possess these tablets, which are decaying in dusty storage.

The texts on the Sumerian tablets are anonymous. Only the Sumerian tablets are anonymous, not the Akkadian tablets. According to the researcher V. Meissner, the Sumerians had a collective perception, aligned with humankind. This means that there was no individuality; they did not perform individual actions, but rather acted as a unified whole. However, this changed when nationalism emerged in Akkad.

This is of utmost importance as it affirms that the Sumerians incorporated everything they observed on numerous occasions, or they adhered to a set of values that remained unaltered, as these values formed the history of their people. Consequently, it was exceedingly challenging for the Sumerians to relate fictional events. They observed something and adapted it to their belief system.

Now we will analyze the key points of the Sumerian pantheon and the Akkadian pantheon. A pantheon is a list of gods held by a religious group or culture such as the Sumerians and Akkadians. Obviously, all cultures have different gods than others, but the Akkadian pantheon and the Sumerian pantheon are incredibly identical because, as we know, the Akkadians absorbed all the customs and gods of the Sumerians. This happened when the Sumerians were about to disappear and the Sumerians merged with the Akkadians.

When the Sumerians merged with the Akkadians, the Sumerians obtained and performed very important tasks with respect to the Akkadian society, as they were very different from the Akkadians. The Akkadians preferred laws and nationalism, and a very great feeling of government arose in them. This destroyed the Sumerian feeling of unity as the Akkadians replaced that by doing the opposite: each individual is different from another, and each one acts differently from another, the population was no longer whole, but each individual was independent. This caused the pantheon of gods to be modified, this made the gods more powerful and divine since the Sumerians believed that their gods lived with them.

For the Sumerians, the gods lived with man. The gods drank with man, talked with man, and ruled the cities of men. For the Akkadians all this was different. For the Akkadians, their gods were in heaven and possessed the power to destroy man.

That is why the Akkadians took a god and turned him into the most powerful god of the existing pantheon. That god was Marduk; later we will talk about this god in more detail.

Now we will talk about the creation myth of the Sumerians and the Akkadians.

The Myth of Creation

In the Sumerian creation myth, everything originated within the Great Absolute Abyss, an abyss of immense magnitude. Many authors who discuss the Anunnaki have theorized that this Great Absolute Abyss may refer to the sky, the stars, and the universe.

Within this abyss, there existed a colossal mountain. When this mountain was destroyed by the god Enlil, heaven and earth came into existence. Several authors suggest that the destruction of this mountain symbolizes matter, the explosion of matter, in other words, the Big Bang. Naturally, there is no concrete evidence to support the idea that the Sumerians were aware of the Big Bang, as it is something that modern science has uncovered. However, the myth indicates that the Great Abyss represents the universe, while the Great Mountain represents matter. Furthermore, the myth elaborates on the creation and existence of the universe.

After Enlil created heaven and earth by demolishing the Great Mountain, other gods brought forth light, darkness, animals, and plants. However, it was the god Enki, along with his helper gods Ninmah and Nammu, who created the first human being. These three gods utilized the mud that resided in the Abzu. The Abzu was a tremendous chasm within the Earth, a vast fissure that connected with the realm

Afterlife or the Underworld.

With the mud of the Abzu, they created human being. Now, in the following chapters, I will explain how these gods created the human being according to the Sumerians and Akkadians.

In the pantheon of Sumerian gods, An is the god of the sky and the father of all gods. It is important to note that An is not Anu, as many may think. Anu is the Akkadian sky god, while An is the Sumerian sky god. Although they represent the same deity, they have different names.

Among the Sumerian gods, we have Enlil, the wind god; Enki, the earth god; Su-en, the moon god; Utu, the sun god; and Inanna, the goddess of life and creation.

Now, let's introduce the secondary gods: Nergal, the lord of the inner world and ruler of Abzu; Ereshkigal, Inanna's sister; Ishkur, the lord of storms; Ninurta, the god of war; and Dumuzi, the god of agriculture.

Now, let us meet the Akkadian gods. The creation and worldview, according to the Akkadians, are different. According to the Akkadians, everything began with water and Abzu. For them, Abzu represented the masculine principle, while the feminine principle was represented by Tiamat. We will discuss these primordial gods in the following chapters. Tiamat who could potentially be a planet according to the texts, is considered a goddess for now. She is believed to have brought forth salt water, as the Akkadians described. The creation of life on Earth occurred through the mixture of salt water and the water in the Abzu, resembling a fertilization of the waters.

However, within this life on Earth, Tiamat and Abzu created two aberrations in the form of serpents: Lahmu and Lahamu. These two serpents instilled fear in humankind and their existence was somewhat obscured in Akkadian records. After the creation of these two aberrations, two gods emerged to govern heaven and earth: Anshar and Kishar.

In the Akkadian pantheon, we now have Anu, who belongs to the Anunnaki race. Anu is the ruling god of heaven according to the Akkadian pantheon, while An is the god of heaven in the Sumerian pantheon. There is also Enlil, the god of the wind, and Ea, who corresponds to Enki in the Sumerian religion. Ea is indeed the god Enki in the Akkadian religion. From now on, whenever I mention Ea, I will be referring to the god of the Akkadians.

There should be no doubt that Ea is Enki. Enki is mentioned in the Sumerian tablets. The Akkadians, due to their cultural changes and assimilation of knowledge, referred to him as Ea. It is important to understand that the Akkadian culture is derived from and influenced by the Sumerian culture. I hope you, my dear reader, have grasped this concept. Your understanding is essential. Please continue reading.

Anu (An), Enlil, and Ea (Enki) divided the created world. They divided life into sections, with each of these gods possessing a fragment of the world. Later, additional gods would emerge, such as Sin, the god of the moon. The list of gods also includes the children of Anu, such as Ishtar, who represents the goddess Venus, and Shamash, the god of the sun. The Akkadians made a significant modification by granting absolute power to the god Marduk, elevating him to the highest divinity. With Marduk as the sole god, the Akkadians established the first monotheistic religion.

Despite introducing the concept of monotheistic religion, the Akkadians still worshipped other gods, with Marduk being the most powerful among them. According to Sumerian tablets, Anu, the most powerful god in Sumerian mythology, transferred his power to Marduk. Marduk's father, Ea (Enki), also relinquished his throne to Marduk. Additionally, Enlil bestowed upon Marduk the Tablets of Destiny, also known as the Me Tablets, which possessed extraordinary powers according to Sumerian mythology.

The possession of the Tablets of Destiny, which represented highly advanced technology, granted the holder unrivaled power among the gods. Enlil entrusted these tablets to Marduk as a result of his victory over Tiamat, an event which I will explain in the upcoming chapters.

The death of the goddess Tiamat signifies a monumental cosmic catastrophe—the collision between two colossal planets: Tiamat and Marduk.

We will explore the details of this event in the subsequent chapters.

It is crucial to mention an important aspect of the Akkadian pantheon: beneath the Abzu, there existed the Kingdom of the Afterlife or Underworld. Those who entered this realm, whether they were humans or gods, would forever wander within the depths of the Earth.

Within this underworld prison resided demons, who played significant roles and featured prominently in the myths of Sumerian and Akkadian tablets. These demons accomplished remarkable feats. The demons dwelling beneath the Abzu hold great importance, and I will delve into their significance in the forthcoming chapters.

Sumerian Tablets

In this chapter, I will talk about the content of the Sumerian tablets, translated by the scholars and researchers Samuel Noah Kramer and Federico Lara Peinado.

In the Sumerian pantheon, we have the Myths of the Origins. In these myths, we find the myth of the Birth of the Moon, where Enlil and Ninlil appear; the myth of the Sumerian Paradise, starring Enki and Ninhursag; the myth of the Problem of Human Creation, starring Enki and Ninma; the myth of the Origin of Cereals; and also, the myth of Vegetables, which tells us about the Origin of Vegetables.

But the most important Sumerian myth is The Sumerian Universal Flood, which tells us how Enlil desires to destroy humankind and Enki tries to prevent that from happening. This myth is found in the first block of Sumerian tablets. We will see more about this in the following chapters.

The Myths of Organization would be the second block of tablets that talk about the Sumerian pantheon. These myths are:

The first myth is The Myth of the Organization of the Planet and the Knowledge regarding Sumer, with Enki being the protagonist.

The myth of Enki and the Creation of a city called E-engurra, which would serve as a temple situated in the Abzu, within the abyss.

The Myth of Enki and the Order of the World is considered the most important myth as it presents the kindness of Enki towards humankind and the power of words. Enki teaches humankind that with words, any war can be ended.

Another myth is The Journey of Inanna and Dumuzi to Nippur.

In the third block of Sumerian tablets, we find the Myths of Human Contact with the Gods. In this block, there is a significant myth called "Inanna and Shu-kale-tuda". This myth tells us about the violation of the goddess Inanna by a human named Shu-kale-tuda. Then, the myth narrates how Inanna sought revenge and unleashed her wrath against humankind, nearly extinguishing it.

This third block of Sumerian tablets also introduces the Myth of the Seven Sumerian Sages. These seven sages were beings created by the Anunnaki and were not human. It is currently unknown what race or species these beings belonged to. However, what is known is that they bestowed knowledge upon humankind, including knowledge of the stars and the gods.

The fourth block of Sumerian tablets contains the Myths of the Heroes, such as Gilgamesh, the king of Uruk, and Lugalbanda, the lord of Aratta.

The fifth block of Sumerian tablets includes the Myths of the Afterlife. These tablets describe the death of Dumuzi, who was captured by demons known as Gallu. These murderous gods or demons resided in the Abzu or beneath it.

In this fifth block of tablets, we also learn about Inanna's descent into the underworld. The tablets in this block also mention the god Lil and the attempts made by some to constantly revive him, to bring him out of the hells. It is curious that the passion for the god Lil bears a striking resemblance to the resurrection of Jesus. I will discuss this in more detail later.

These are the Sumerian tablets that tell us about the mythology of this ancient civilization. Let's see now the Akkadian tablets that tell us about the myths of the Akkadians.

Akkadian Tablets

As we know, the Akkadians copied all the Sumerian texts, exported them to their geographical terrain, and modified them due to the rise of nationalism. This resulted in the supreme leader, Marduk, becoming the god of all Anunnaki. Let us study the Akkadian tablets in detail in the following blocks.

First Block: Marduk being the only god for the Akkadians, the religion of this civilization would become monotheistic in the future. Thus, the Akkadian myths would begin. The first myths in this block of Sumerian tablets are the Creation Myths, including the Origin of Everything: Enûma Eliš or Enuma Elish.

Second Block: Akkadian tablets also narrate the Creation of Man. Ea (Enki) creates the human being from the blood of a rebel god called Kingu. According to the Akkadians, humans were born with the blood of a god. We are children of Kingu. Additionally, we find the myth of the Lamga gods.

Third Block: These tablets tell us about the *Myths of the Wars*. The most famous myth is the myth of the *Anzû Bird*. This evil bird only wanted to steal the Tablets of Destiny (better known as the Me Tablets) in order to defeat all the Anunnaki gods. However, this bird was defeated by the god Ninurta. There are more war myths, such as *The Wars of Gilgamesh, Ishtar,* *and the Iron Bull,* or better known as the Celestial Bull. The Myth of Ishtar and the Iron Bull is particularly famous. Many believe that the Iron Bull represents a form of technology since the tablets mention that it shoots lightning bolts. We will explore this further in the following chapters.

This group of tablets also provides information about Tiamat and suggests a great cosmic cataclysm resulting from the collision of two large planets.

Fourth Block: These tablets contain myths of Destruction and Salvation, including the Universal Flood. The Universal Flood is narrated from the perspective of the Akkadians. The tablets also tell the myth of Atra-Hasis, who is the Akkadian version of Noah. Atra-Hasis in Akkadian, Ziusudra in Sumerian, Utnapishtim in Babylonian, and Noah in the Bible are all the same person. According to the Akkadian tablets, Atra-Hasis was a man who built a large ship, an ark filled with animals, and the great flood was the reason for constructing the ark. This myth existed in Akkadian civilization 3500 years before the birth of Christ.

I mentioned Babylon earlier. Babylon, like Assyria, emerged in different timelines and histories compared to Akkad. These civilizations arose after the rise of Akkad. Therefore, the chronological appearance of these civilizations in history is as follows: Sumer, Akkad, Babylon, Assyria (with the last two civilizations being closely related in time), and other cultures. However, it is in Sumer and Akkad where the real history of humankind is concentrated.

In the myths of Destruction and Salvation, we also encounter the myth of Erra. Erra was a god who sought to completely destroy Babylon under the command of the supreme god Marduk.

Fifth Block: Here we find the Myths of Ultratomb. This group of tablets tells us about Nergal and Ereshkigal. These myths depict the lives of these two gods who were united in marriage and resided in the underworld. The tablets also narrate the descent of Ishtar (the Akkadian goddess) into the underworld. This descent is identical to Inanna's descent into the underworld in Sumerian culture.

The tablets in the fifth block also relate to the myth of the Vision of the Inner World and the Plant of Immortality of Gilgamesh, which is a beautiful and well-known myth.

Additionally, the group of tablets includes the myths of The Ascension, where we find the myth of Adapa. Adapa was a created man who was superior to regular humans and sought immortality. Another myth present in this block of tablets is the myth of Atana, who desired to travel to the heavens with the gods to obtain the plant of birth.

Sixth Block: In this group of tablets, we encounter the Myths of Exaltation. One important myth in this category is *The 50 Names of Marduk*, which extols the power of the Anunnaki god Marduk.

Sumerian Universal Flood

I will try to give you a proper understanding of this Sumerian myth, dear reader, as it is exceedingly challenging to explain it adequately in words.

The Sumerian flood found on a tablet, in the city of Nippur, is the first narration in the history of a Universal Flood. The background of the text, which repeats ancient oral traditions, was later adapted into other religious and even historical myths.

Significantly, a considerable portion of this myth remains unknown, as 70% of the entire text is missing. However, when the decipherable content emerges, these texts recount the presence of a divine being who speaks of rescuing humankind from annihilation.

The text makes mention of the following:

"A flood will inundate all the peoples, all the temples of worship so as to destroy the seed of humankind... It is the decision of the gods An, Enlil, and Ninhursag. The destruction of the throne".

From here, more than 40 lines of text appear to be destroyed, where one could have found the instructions given to Ziusudra, the biblical Noah. Let us continue reading:

"All storms and tempests were immediately unleashed. The Flood inundated temples of worship. After the Flood flooded the whole earth for 7 days and 7 nights, and the huge boat sailed on the waters, Utu emerged and illuminated the sky and the

earth. Ziusudra opened one of the windows of the ark, and the mighty god Utu cast his powerful thunderbolts into the gigantic boat. King Ziusudra knelt before the god Utu. Ziusudra sacrificed oxen and lambs in his honor. "All of you shall invoke for the earth," said Utu, "... that An and Enlil created all the animals that are on the earth." Ziusudra bowed his head on the ground to bow to An and Enlil. An and Enlil protected King Ziusudra, gave him the life of a god, and there descended toward Ziusudra the strong breath of a god. Then Ziusudra, the king, who saved mankind of that age, received the blessing of the gods who took him to live in the east of the seas, in Dilmun, where he would live forever."

The rest of the text was lost. Almost 39 lines of the text were completely lost in time.

Ziusudra, the biblical Noah. Noah, Ziusudra, and Atra-Hasis are the same person. They are the same person! They all do the same thing: build a big boat to save themselves from the Universal Flood. The authors, Samuel Noah Kramer and Federico Lara Peinado, suggest that we read Genesis in the Bible, verse 6:8, because what we will find in the Bible is exactly the same as what is recounted in the Sumerian tablets, whose age is over 3000 years, these tablets were written more than 3000 years before Christ!

So what does all of this signify? What does it mean that this Sumerian myth, recorded on ancient tablets, predates the Bible itself? Well, it suggests the possibility that all of this may have actually happened.

Why would two cultures and religions, separated by vast distances of time and space, share the same narrative? These questions provoke deep contemplation. There is a concealed secret here, and I am determined to pursue it until I uncover the truth.

-Samuel Noah Kramer translated this: *"The thunderbolt of the gods' fury sacrificed and burned a single ram."*

-Federico Lara Peinado translated the following: *"The thunderbolt motivated by the fury of the gods, sacrificed and burned several rams".*

With this, I aim to demonstrate that these authors are highly meticulous when it comes to directly translating the tablets. A mere plural has become a subject of annotation in this book, and I believe it to be of great significance as it provides us with a basis for further investigation.

You can read Sitchin's inventions to better understand the Anunnaki myth, but understand that Federico Lara Peinado, Samuel Noah Kramer, and Anton Parks have different viewpoints. I dare say that their translations are more accurate and better translated than Sitchin's translations.

Anunnaki in Sumerian Tablets

The gods of the stars, the Anunnaki, appear in Sumerian mythology. However, in the texts of the Sumerian tablets, something else emerges: humanoid beings born from the depths of the ocean, serpents that cast enormous shadows upon the earth. These serpents are called Usumgal.

In these texts, devices called Me Tablets also appear. These tablets had the ability to build or destroy the universe.

In this chapter, we will gain a much better understanding of these facts.

In the data I have collected, I have found interesting and significant events. I will discuss the creation of the human being and also delve into strange indications that there could have been advanced technology in ancient times, the gold of the Anunnaki, monstrosities, and other beings. Additionally, I will explore the significance of the serpent figure, as it also exists in Sumerian culture. Lastly, I will save something truly mysterious and unexpected for the end—a surprise for you, dear reader.

This last piece of information has left me deeply disturbed because it is something very unknown. This information delves deeply into the Me Tablets, the Tablets of Destiny. In this book, we will discuss this seemingly highly advanced technology in greater detail. I will talk about Sumerian myths because the Akkadians are a copy of the Sumerians, so the data is the same for both cultures. Here, I have created a list of interesting facts:

Fact 1: The Origin and Creation of Human Being

In this tablet, we will find the myth of Enki and Ninhursag. Here we can find the following fragment:

"-My brother, what is it that hurts you?
-My rib is what hurts me.
-I have made Ninti be born for you."

The Akkadian word "Ti" means "rib," but in Sumerian, it also means "life." So, when Ninti is mentioned, it means "Lady of the Rib" or "Lady of Life." Here, we see a clear example of a great parallelism with the Bible and Genesis: God created the first woman, Eve, the mother of life, from Adam's rib. It is impressive that Sumerian culture refers to the rib as a symbol of creation.

Now, let's delve into the next myth, the myth of Lahar and Ashnan. This myth reveals the following:

"At the beginning of creation, men did not know how to eat bread, they did not know how to wear clothes, men walked on their hands and on their feet, they ate plants with their mouths as well as sheep. They drank water from the holes in the ground".

This refers to the hominids that existed on Earth before man. These hominids were like chimpanzees, they walked on hands and feet. But the question I ask myself here is, how did the Sumerians know that man is descended from the primate? How is it that all this invention exists, since supposedly all this is mythology? Or did the ancient Sumerians write on Sumerian tablets what their gods dictated to them? Let us continue reading the myth of Lahar and Ashnan.

"In the enclosure, they, for prosperity, caused to exist in people the breath of life."

This passage means the knowledge and science that the gods bestowed upon humankind. In the Greek myth of Prometheus, Prometheus stole the gods' knowledge to share it with humans. All cultures discuss the leap of evolution, a transition towards infinity, the conscious step that transforms a hominid into a human being.

Federico Lara Peinado highlights that the gods needed something to work with. In other words, Sumerian mythology reveals how the gods created human beings and facilitated the genetic evolution from hominids to humans. This was the process of creation.

Fact 2: Organization Myths

These myths tell us about Enki and the Order of the World. Let us analyze the following text:

"He spread his shadow over the globe."

How is this possible? How is it possible that the Sumerians knew that the Earth was round? In the

Middle Ages, it was known that the Earth was flat. How is it possible that 3400 years before Christ the Sumerians knew that the Earth was an ovoid globe?

The Sumerians believed in four elements that shaped existence: the sky, the wind, the water, and the earth. The sky represented the universe, or space, and its god was An, known as Anu in Akkadian. The wind symbolized the atmosphere, and its god was Enlil. The sea was represented by Ea, known as Enki in Sumerian, who was both the god of the sea and the god of the earth for the Sumerians.

Beneath the earth, below the Abzu, which is the abyss of the world, lay the underworld. This underworld bears similarities to the underworld in Greek culture and the concept of hell in the Bible. Once someone entered the underworld, whether human or god, they could never leave. Escape from the underworld was impossible.

The underworld is described as a place of numerous horrors and curses. One of them is the Horror of Eternity. Let us continue our analysis of these texts.

"Enki, the king of Abzu, commanded the fates: 'black earth let all your trees be tall.'"

The Sumerian people used the term "Meluhha" to refer to what we now know as the Black Earth. Even to this day, the geographical origin of the Sumerians remains unknown, as we are unsure of where they originated from. However, I had previously encountered the phrase "Black Earth" while studying tablets. It is interesting to note that the Egyptian word for Egypt, "Kemet", also translates to Black Earth.

The fact that both Egypt and the ancient Sumerian region share the same meaning, referring to Black Earth, raises an intriguing question. How is it possible that Egypt and the geographical area of ancient Sumer have this similarity in their names? This could be a mere coincidence, but to truly comprehend this intriguing connection, a more thorough and comprehensive study is required. Let's continue our analysis of the text in greater detail.

"To the lady who procreates, the breath of the country, the life of the black heads".

According to Francisco Lara Peinado, this reference does not pertain to Africans or the black race, but rather to the hair on the heads of human beings. Humans, considered the creation of the Anunnaki, were referred to as "black heads" because the Anunnaki observed them from the sky. This leads me to speculate that the Anunnaki themselves may have been hairless. While seemingly insignificant, this detail could potentially provide clues about the appearance of these Anunnaki deities.

If the Anunnaki were indeed hairless, they would have been bald. This connection brings to mind the snakes that will be discussed later, which is another intriguing fact considering their presence in various world religions.

This second set of facts, labeled as fact number 2, proves highly interesting. It sheds light on the origin of human beings and the Sumerians' perception of the Order of the World. These valuable insights can be derived from the tablets of Lahar and Ashnan, Enki and the Founding of E-engurra, Enki and the Order of the World, and Enki and Ninhursag.

Fact 3: Technology and Science

In the myth of origins known as Lahar and Ashnan, which recounts the gods' bestowal of cereal, specifically wheat, upon humankind, there exists a fragment of text that reads as follows:

"When in the mountain of heaven and earth An created the Anunnaki gods, and as Ashnan had not yet been born, he had not yet been formed."

Let's analyze this: prior to the creation of heaven and earth, and even before the formation of our planet, there existed only one mountain floating in space within the cosmos. This mountain was believed to be the origin from which the Anunnaki emerged. Various authors suggest that this mountain might have served as the dwelling place for the Anunnaki. It is comparable to a mode of transportation, possibly a ship or a machine, because if the planet Earth had not yet been created, what existed in its place?

In the myths concerning the Order of the World, specifically in the myth of Enki and the founding of E-engurra (the temple that Enki sought to establish on the waters of the Abzu), we encounter the following text:

"Your bolt has no equal, your hinge is a monstrous lion, your cornices are the celestial bull, artistic adornment of the wall".

According to Francisco Lara Peinado, the Celestial Bull is a mythological being created by Anu. This bull is a being that appeared in the epic poem of Gilgamesh. Many authors have associated this Celestial Bull with a machine, a guardian that would be in the sky protecting several unknown things, as seen in the epic poem of Gilgamesh where this Celestial Bull appears defending a cave.

In the myths of the Organization, specifically in the myth of Enki and the Order of the World, we are told how Enki attempts to bring order to his land, which has been bestowed upon him.

Let us analyze the following text:

"After returning from his visit to that place, after Enki, the father, had carried it over the Euphrates, he caused the waters to increase and lengthened their fertility. He also filled the Tigris with running water".

This fragment describes how Enki was able to channel, direct, and guide the Euphrates and Tigris rivers. I have heard many authors suggest that Enki employed human labor to build mines. However, an alternate version states that Enki utilized human beings to control the flow of the Tigris and Euphrates rivers.

The text does not explicitly state whether Enki personally carried out the task or employed human beings to manage the waters of the Euphrates and

Tigris rivers.

Another fragment on the same tablet is as follows:

"Enki built a temple at the bottom of the sea, whose interior is artistic".

According to Francisco Lara Peinado, there are no interesting facts in this text. However, I would like to express the following opinion: there are many civilizations that have built their temples at the bottom of the sea. Every time I come across this concept, it strongly reminds me of the stories by H.P. Lovecraft about beings from the stars who constructed a temple in the sea. I am aware that there is no direct connection between the American horror writer and the Anunnaki myth. It may seem far-fetched, but the idea of building temples at the bottom of the sea could potentially be associated with Atlantis.

Please note that this is solely my personal opinion. We currently lack scientific evidence to establish any direct relationship between these concepts. It is merely a coincidence I wanted to highlight.

Fact 4: The Anunnaki Gold

Zecharia Sitchin consistently mentioned that gold was essential for the reconstruction of the atmosphere on the planet Nibiru. Nibiru, a nomadic planet with a 3600-year orbit where the Anunnaki allegedly resided and originated from, was the reason why they came to Earth. Their purpose was to create humankind and utilize them as labor for gold extraction.

However, the texts found in the Sumerian tablets present a stark contrast to the fictional narrative constructed by Sitchin. In the myths of the Organization, specifically in the tablet of Enki and E-engurra, we encounter the following information:

"The gods said goodbye to lord Nudimmud and said, 'There he has built the holy house with lapis lazuli, and with the magnificence of gold he has covered and adorned it'."

In other words, Enki possessed an abundance of gold, to the extent that he covered and adorned the palace of E-engurra with it. Now, dear reader, which scenario appears more credible to you? Rebuilding an atmosphere with gold or utilizing gold to embellish an entire temple?

Another reference to gold in the myths of the Organization, specifically in the myth of Enki and the Order of the World, provides the following account:

"The magilum ships carried gold and silver to Nippur, for the king of all lands, Enki."

Another fragment of text about gold in Sumerian culture:

"Nidaba, the lord of the boat, delivers a golden scepter to the lord."

As we can see, gold exists in Sumerian history as an offering of great value to the gods. So Sitchin invented a fictitious story about gold. The truth is in the Sumerian tablets. Let's continue analyzing more texts.

Fact 5: Monstrosities and other creatures

The Anunnaki not only created humans, but they also brought forth demons. In the myths of the Organization, specifically in the tablet of Enki and the founding of E-engurra, there exists a fragment of text that mentions the following:

"When Enki stood up, the fishes also stood up raising their hands in prayer."

How is it possible that the fishes raised their hands in prayer to Enki? Did the fishes at that time have arms?

These fishes with hands are also found in the Dogon culture. The Dogon said that the Nommos (beings with physical characteristics of fishes, amphibians, and snakes) had arms and that they came down from the stars and gave their knowledge to man. The same as the Sumerians narrated but in another era.

In the myths of the Organization, exactly in the tablet of Enki and the Order of the World, we can read:

"Kulla, the great clay kneader of the whole country".

This tablet tells us that Kulla was a second-class god created by Enki whose work was the repair of the temples. With this we prove that Enki was a god capable of creating life, he had the power to create other beings to fulfill his personal goals by obeying his orders. The word "order" has a hidden meaning since it is related to the Me Tablets, and the Me Tablets are what will really fascinate you like me, reader. We will talk about them later.

Sumerian Snakes

Were the Anunnaki reptilians or were they human-like beings? That is the big question we will resolve in this chapter.

The first finding that suggests the Anunnaki were reptilian beings comes from the earliest Sumerian settlement, dating back over 5000 years before Christ. This predates the existence of the Sumerian civilization, indicating the presence of a pre-Sumerian era. Sumerian figurines provide evidence of the appearance of these reptilian beings. Notably, there is a figurine depicting a humanoid reptilian being breastfeeding a small chimeric creature with a humanoid body and a reptilian head.

Obviously, the concept of a reptile breastfeeding a chimera, a hybrid of reptile and mammal, may seem illogical and unusual. However, there are additional clues suggesting that these beings were indeed reptilian. The Anunnaki beings are not the sole representatives of reptilian entities; there is another term that should be remembered: Usumgal. In my book, *"Anunnaki: Reptilians in the History of Humankind,"* I explore the idea that these Usumgal beings constitute another reptilian race.

According to the myths of the Organization, specifically mentioned in the tablet "Enki and the Founding of E-engurra," the following information is provided about the Usumgal beings:

"He brought terror down to the great river, and thus the south wind came to violently disturb the Euphrates. Its rudder was Nirah."

According to Francisco Lara Peinado, the being known as Usumgal was a colossal serpent with a demonic appearance. The Sumerians held a deep fear of this serpent, referred to as Nirah.

Another noteworthy mention on this tablet is the curse known as the South Wind. This curse was devised by An (known as Anu to the Akkadians), a Sumerian god. It consisted of four winds: the south wind, the north wind, the east wind, and the west wind. This curse brought about destruction and calamities. It is speculated that the manifestations of this curse could be hurricanes, typhoons, or similar calamities. However, what remains certain is that all Sumerians dreaded Nirah, the demonic serpent, and the four winds unleashed by An.

In the myths of the Organization, specifically in the tablet "Enki and the Order of the World," the following text can be found:

"Great Dragon who lives in Eridu, your shadow covers the sky and the earth."

Are we talking about huge snakes that leave their shadows on the ground while floating and flying through the air? Are they the celestial houses, the ships of the Anunnaki? Or maybe these huge snakes could be beings that accompanied the Anunnaki?

This constant reference to huge snakes and dragons that were in the sky, at the beginning of the eras, also exists in other civilizations. Let's continue analyzing the texts:

"The divine Usumgal of the sky, the great friend of An, Enki put him in charge."

There is a difference between the Usumgal and the Anunnaki gods. According to Francisco Lara Peinado, Usumgal means "Great Dragon" or "Great Serpent."

When it refers to the "friend of An," we can observe that the Sumerians differentiated between the Anunnaki race and the Usumgal. The Usumgal were often depicted as powerful serpents or dragons. Further exploration of this subject will be presented in subsequent chapters.

The Tablets of Destiny

The Tablets of Destiny, or Me tablets, are the most interesting thing about the Anunnaki. In the myths of the Organization, specifically in the Tablets of Enki and the Order of the World, there is a text that says the following:

"Great prince, lord of abundance, lord of intelligence, lord whom An loves, you perform tasks and make decisions with efficiency since you are an expert and know the destinies."

The word "destiny" in Sumerian means Me. Me refers to orders or laws that can destroy or create creation. Let's keep reading:

"My father, king of the universe, made me shine in the sky and on earth. My elder brother, the king of all countries in the world, gathered all the rules and placed them all in my right hand."

This text talks about Enki, the Anunnaki god who holds a Me tablet in his right hand. The Sumerians may be referring to the magic or technology that these gods possessed.

Samuel Noah Kramer in his book, "History Begins at Sumer," explains the meaning of the Me tablets a little better. According to him, if the texts on these tablets were read, the tablets could be activated to create or destroy life according to Sumerian tablets.

This reminds me of a lot of some software. In other words, if a programmer creates software with a list of orders undoubtedly the software will obey those orders. What if we were software created to fulfill orders from these Anunnaki gods?

The tablets talk a lot about battles to obtain the Me tablets. In the Babylonian tablets, Marduk, the most powerful god of all (even more powerful than Enki, Enlil, and An), takes possession of the Me tablets. With these tablets, Marduk can create and destroy anything.

The fact that Enki has inscriptions or orders written on these Me tablets which were on his arm like a bracelet, makes me imagine that it is a type of device that attaches to the arm and can create or destroy things using very advanced technology. But that is just my invention. I only read what the Sumerian tablets say, and that is my conclusion.

The objective of this book is to present the content of the Sumerian tablets without interpretation so that you, the reader, can investigate more about this and draw your own conclusions.

The Seven Sages

In the Sumerian tablets, we also find the myth of the Seven Sages or Seven Wise Men, beings who, in ancient times, gathered all the knowledge of the gods to distribute it to all the peoples of the world. These wise men had two-thirds of Anunnaki DNA. Even the myth written on these tablets ends with a strange spell or enchantment of a completely unknown origin and effect, a meaning that not even Francisco Lara Peinado or Samuel Noah Kramer have been able to decipher.

The myth of the Seven Sage is one of the most important myths of Sumerian culture. The tablets where these myths were written mixed Sumerian culture with Akkadian culture. This is because the fragments of these tablets were found south of Nineveh and were mixed together. That is, Sumerian texts and Akkadian texts were found in one place by archaeologists.

We must remember that the Akkadians copied everything from the Sumerians including the Sumerian texts to adapt them to their time and needs. The content of these texts tells us about the existence of seven ancient sages who referred to ascended humans. What does this mean? It means that for the Akkadians the Anunnaki, especially Ea (Enki), created seven demigods by mixing the DNA of humans with the DNA of the gods. These seven wise men had much more intelligence and knowledge than the people Enki had previously created.

One of the seven sages, the wisest of all, Adapa, was the first to ascend to the heavens and learn about the gods and their knowledge. When he returned to Earth he told mankind about it. It is even believed that the scribes, the ones who wrote the Sumerian tablets were based on what one of these sages told. But this tablet ends in a very mysterious way. This tablet concludes with a strange spell or enchantment made by these Seven Sages whose purpose is unknown. It is one of the few tablets in which a complete spell appears. We will analyze this later.

Now let us study the myth of the Seven Sages in more depth. Let us read the following text:

"The first sage was Adapa, who purified Eridu and ascended to the heavens."

We must emphasize here the word "sage". In the ancient world there has always existed the figure of the sages who granted knowledge to man. Perhaps these sages were the means for the gods to communicate with men. The Seven Sages were created by Enki. In the following pages we will learn the names of these sages. I want to warn you that Sage Number Seven is a complete mystery since his name is still unknown.

I have already mentioned Adapa, one of the greatest sages of all time who ascended to the heavens and lived with the Anunnaki gods. There is a tablet that narrates the myth of Adapa, but we will see and analyze this tablet in the following chapters since it is a very extensive tablet with a lot of data to analyze.

The full name of Adapa is Umanna Adapa, which means *"the wise man born of the sea."* The Babylonians referred to Adapa as Oannes in their tablets, which is the fish man who gave knowledge to humankind in Babylonian myths. Adapa, also known as Adam, was created by Enki who was considered the God of Wisdom in ancient Sumerian culture.

The similarity in etymology between Adapa and Adam, and the parallelism between their stories, is a topic of great interest. This parallelism raises the question of what the true history of humankind is. According to antiquity and history, the Sumerian texts are much older than the Bible.

If we assume that Adapa and Adam are the same person, then many things begin to make sense. For example, in the Sumerian text, *"The wise men, perfect puradu fishes of the seas, are seven."*

Perfect paradu fishes, is it possible that they are related to the figures of fishes? We have already seen in previous chapters the relationship with the big fishes. But why are the big fishes related to these sages? Did they have a snake-like, scaly aspect? Every time I go deeper and deeper into the depths of the knowledge that exists in these Sumerian tablets, all of this makes me think that everything is oriented to the fact that these wise men had an aspect of scaly fish, of serpents...

The wise men resembled fish men just like the

Dogon who also spoke of these Nommos, these fish beings. But let's continue, we know that there are seven wise men, but here there is something really important. Federico Lara Peinado collects an annotation where not 7 wise men are described, but 10 wise men. These 10 sages existed before these 7 sages. These 10 wise men ruled the Earth for 430,000 years, 430,000 years before the Universal Flood!

If Federico Lara Peinado, a great scholar who dedicated more than 30 years of his life to the study of these Sumerian tablets, mentions that there is a period of 430,000 years where these 10 wise men ruled the world, then this means that the history of the Anunnaki written on the Sumerian tablets is worth investigating.

Apparently, I will have to do some research and write a new book to find out who these 10 sages were. These sages existed 430,000 years ago before the Flood, a huge and very distant amount of time. So, if this is true, that means we must travel to the times of Telentia, Atlantis, Lemuria, and Hyperborea. These lost continents for which there is evidence that they really existed once.

It is possible that the Sumerians were not the world's first civilization, nor were the Proto-Sumerians. It is possible that before these civilizations, there were more unofficial civilizations. For science, it is very possible that this was the case.

Let us know the names of the seven sages: Adapa, Nunpiriggaldin, Piriggalnungal, Piriggalabzu, Lu-

Nanna, Eninkarnunna, and the seventh sage whose name is a mystery. According to Francisco Lara Peinado, he theorizes that it could have been Enki. However, in the tablets it is mentioned that Enki created the seven sages, so it is impossible that Enki created himself. Therefore, only the names of six sages are known, and the identity of the seventh sage will remain a mystery. The tablet is destroyed almost at the end, and we will discuss this in the next chapters. There is an incantation, but at the end of this destroyed tablet, we cannot read who the seventh sage was.

Let us continue analyzing the Sumerian texts about the seven wise men:

"Piriggalabzu, born in Eridu, and who set his seal on a suhur-mash fish, angered Ea very much in the Abzu, and Ea cut off all the cords of his cervical spine."

We should remember that we are mixing the tablets of the Sumerians and the tablets of the Akkadians which is why Ea is Akkadian while Enki is Sumerian.

When we talk about cutting his cervical vertebra, we are talking about reducing his intelligence. Enki (Ea) was the creator of the sages, so he endowed them a higher degree of intelligence and knowledge, which was almost similar to that of the Anunnaki gods. This sage, Piriggalabzu, does something that arouses the fury of Ea (Enki), and Enki grants him a punishment: the reduction of the gift of extreme knowledge.

Let us continue analyzing these texts:

"The fourth sage was Lu-Nanna, wise only by two-thirds,

who helped a ushumgallu dragon to flee from the Eninkarnunna of Ishtar, palace of king Shulgi. The rest of the sages were born as humans to whom the god Ea gifted perfect and vast knowledge."

First, we find Lu-Nanna, the fourth sage, whose genes contained 20% human genes and 80% god genes. In other words, the Sumerians had knowledge of hybridization, the creation of chimeric beings created from Anunnaki DNA and human DNA. These hybrid beings are mentioned in the Bible and are better known as Nephilim or Giants, which are also mentioned in the Book of Enoch.

We have mentioned the word Usumgal, which is spelled ushumgallu. According to the text we have just read, it mentions this ushumgallu being, a dragon-like being that escapes from the temple of the goddess Ishtar (Inanna for the Sumerians). This ushumgallu or Usumgal is a reptilian race that coexisted with the Anunnaki. But there is an even more interesting hypothesis: the Usumgal would be a kind of vehicle that transported the Anunnaki. In many texts, references to the word Usumgal are mentioned. The Usumgal always appeared when men saw elongated shadows on the ground, that is when the Anunnaki flew in these Usumgal. When these texts mention that these Usumgal came out of the temples. Perhaps these temples could be garages where these Usumgal were waiting for their passengers to fly out of these garages? This hypothesis comes from the Sumerian texts.

This tablet, which narrates the existence of the Seven Wise Men, ends with a strange and mysterious incantation that has no concordance with other tablets. According to Federico Lara Peinado, the incantation mentions the Seven Sumerian Wise Men.

If these Seven Sages really existed and performed many spells and incantations for an unknown purpose, what effect would these incantations have?

Mesopotamia

Describing the history of Mesopotamia is extremely complicated, as it was home to many civilizations with completely opposite origins, different languages, religions, and traditions that converged and fought among themselves. Therefore, before explaining the chronological events of the different civilizations that interacted in Mesopotamia since the origin of human civilization, I will make a list of all the civilizations that interacted with each other and later had great importance in our study of the Sumerian texts and all the misunderstandings that have been created.

The list of civilizations includes:
-Sumer
-Akkadia
-Babylonian (whose history unfolded in different periods with moments of booms and busts in which the Babylonians interacted with other civilizations)
-Assyria
-Hittite
-Mitanni
-And Persian.

Now let's travel 5500 years before Christ when the first villages began developing in the area. In these villages, for the first time, social differentiation began to develop through social stratification, as well as a slightly centralized administration and first commercialization at the local level. The villages of Eridu and Ubaid were part of this period.

Moving forward to 3500 BC, these villages began developing into cities during the Ubaid and Eridu periods. These civilizations were stratified, with a social hierarchy, a large population, public architecture, a centralized administration, and long-distance trade. Here we can find characteristics that have defined our present complex civilization, and it is here where we will begin to talk about the mysterious people known as the Sumerians. First of all, we must situate this world geographically. The Sumerian civilization was supposedly located south of Mesopotamia.

But before we talk about Sumer, we must ask ourselves, where did these people come from? What is their origin? Who are the Sumerians? This is a much-debated topic in archaeology and history. Many scholars do not really know their origin. However, archaeology has many theories concerning this mystery. The oldest theory suggests that the origin of the Sumerians would be in the north or east of Mesopotamia, in the mountainous areas or the interior of Iraq.

More Myhts

The Journey of Nanna to Nippur
This myth tells us about the importance of Nanna's journey with regard to the power of the great god Enlil. This myth is not complete, but we know that Nanna gave his blessing to Enlil, giving him power and exalting him. Let's analyze the following text:

"Nanna-Suen anchored his celestial boat."

This celestial boat has clear references to a vehicle, celestial boats that the Anunnaki used for travel. We can also see this in Indian mythology with the Vimanas. These flying vehicles appear in the texts of the Mahabharata, the Ramayana, and the Rigveda. Indian texts were younger than Sumerian texts and speak exactly the same thing: devices whose purpose was the transportation and travel of the gods through the heavens.

Nanna means man of the sky. This Anunnaki god is also known as Nanna-Suen. Suen is a Sumerian symbol that means moon. So Nanna is the name of a sky god associated with the moon. Nanna is a Sumerian god, but the Akkadians call him Sin.

Dumuzi and Enkimdu
In this tablet, we find the myth of the courtship between two gods, Dumuzi and Enkimdu, who both court the goddess Inanna (known as Ishtar to the Akkadians). This myth is important because it has a

parallel with the story of Cain and Abel. One fragment reads:

"The maiden is Inanna, in the stable, the maiden of the sheepfold..."

This story has much to analyze. Inanna (Ishtar for the Akkadians) was the wife of An (Anu for the Akkadians), the god of the heavens and all Anunnaki. Thus, Inanna was considered the owner of the heavens.

Dumuzi and Enkimdu both competed for the love of Inanna. Dumuzi's name was originally Dumuzi-Abzu, the legitimate son of the Abzu, which connected the earth to the underworld. This myth tells us that Dumuzi was the protagonist, but he died at some point. In the Akkadian period, he was revived. Thanks to Ishtar, the protagonist of the myth of the Descent of Ishtar into the Underworld, we know that it was this goddess who revived the old, dead god.

Samuel Noah Kramer even dares to link this event with the resurrection of Jesus Christ, which is unsettling because the Bible draws heavily from ancient Sumerian texts.

There are many similarities between the myth of Dumuzi and Enkimdu and the biblical story of Cain and Abel, more than we realize. Dumuzi and Enkimdu were gods of cattle herders, while Cain and Abel were sheepherders who fought to the death with Cain emerging as the victor and a murderer. These stories are essentially the same but with different names.

Emesh and Eten

These tablets tell us about the importance of summer and winter for human beings. This myth tells us about how Enlil assigned on Earth what winter should do and what summer should do. There is an interesting text in the Sumerian tablets that says:

"Emesh gave his brother much gold, all the silver, and the beautiful lapis lazuli."

Every time I find the word gold in Sumerian tablets, they destroy all the invented stories of Zecharia Sitchin since he said that gold was very scarce on the planet of the Anunnaki and that they needed to extract gold from Earth to repair the atmosphere of their legendary planet Nibiru.

Now we know that gold was abundant and gifts were made with gold, even among the Anunnaki. So gold was not a product that the Anunnaki gods needed.

We must mention that Nibiru does not appear in the Sumerian tablets either. There is a small reference in the Enuma Elish myth (the Origin of Everything) but the Enuma Elish is not a Sumerian myth, it is Babylonian. So the Enuma Elish myth is a copy of a copy of a copy that distorted the true story written by the Sumerians to adapt to the times of Babylonian civilization.

So now you know, you should understand better that Zecharia Sitchin lied. His books are important and great for a science fiction movie but that's all it is: fiction and lies. The truth is in the Sumerian tablets.

Inanna and Shukallituda

This myth tells us how Inanna becomes angry with a mortal human who rapes her while she is in a deep sleep. Inanna was sleeping, and after this, she unleashes her anger by brutally punishing humankind and killing many humans. The text reads as follows:

"When Inanna crossed the skies and the earth, after crossing Elam and Shubur, and after crossing mountains, she was a hierodule. Inanna who was tired rested her body in the garden and slept. Shukallituda, a gardener, watched her from the other side of the great garden and violated her, taking her in his strong arms. Then, Shukallituda returned to the other side of the garden."

Hierodule is a word that means goddess or woman who practiced prostitution in sacred temples.

The story may not make complete sense: a goddess who descends from the heavens to rest in a garden and starts sleeping, only for a human to appear and rape her, after which he flees. However, let's continue reading:

"The dawn disappeared and the sun appeared. The sleeping woman woke up and saw with terror around her..."

Inanna is no longer a goddess, but now a woman. This makes us think that the Anunnaki gods were not entirely divine beings, but lived among human beings. They ate, drank, and slept with human beings. However, this changes in the Akkadian tablets, where the gods were invisible and lived in the sky. Let's continue analyzing the Sumerian text:

"All the wells were filled with blood, all the forests, and all the beautiful gardens were filled with blood. Those who searched for firewood at that time drank blood, and the serving women filled the buckets only with blood. 'I want to know the name of the one who abused my beautiful being. I will search for him in all the nations of the Earth.'"

This myth is interesting to analyze because it tells us important things about the gods. For the Sumerians, the gods were physical beings, but their consciousness and technology were much more advanced. Thus, we can conclude that they were not divine gods, but beings like us.

They were extraterrestrial beings since they came from the sky and the stars. This changes in the Akkadian texts, and the change is even greater in the Babylonian texts where Marduk becomes the only all-powerful god of the Anunnaki surpassing An, Enlil, and Enki in power. We will discuss this in the following chapters.

Sumerian People

This civilization was in the desert but there were other civilizations around it. These civilizations were feeding and developing near the fruits of the Tigris and Euphrates, the two rivers where Sumerian culture developed.

The cities of Aššur and Mari were some of the few civilizations that interacted with Sumer commercially, but as an empire, it was the Akkadians who were also located to the south of Mesopotamia, making the city of Kish the geographical boundary.

What was the relationship between the Akkadians and the Sumerians? Well, this relationship was a constant cultural exchange. At first, Sumerian culture was superior, but at some point, the Akkadian empire absorbed all their knowledge, culture, customs, and religion, effectively swallowing up Sumeria.

This civilization resurfaced with what is known as the Neo-Sumerian period, with the Third Dynasty of Ur that can be dated from around 2192 BC. This moment in Sumerian civilization concludes with the invasion of the Martu people (or Amorites) in 2004 BC.

After this, we must ask ourselves, what civilizations were around Sumer and Akkad? We find the beginning of the Babylonians, known as the Paleo-Babylonian Empire. Here we have a great hegemony. On the one hand, this Paleo-Babylonian Empire is characterized as Amorite (the Amorites belonged to a people close to the Paleo-Babylonian Empire). On the other hand, we have the hegemony of two other cities that we can see on the map of Mesopotamia: Isin and Larsa. Isin appeared first, then Larsa. Isin appeared in 2000 BC, and Larsa in 1932 BC.

At the same time as this Paleo-Babylonian Empire and the hegemony of Isin and Larsa, we find what would later be the Assyrian Empire, that is, the Ancient Assyrian Empire. All of this happens because Aššur installs a dynasty with Akkadian names that begins to battle with neighboring civilizations and begins to have preeminence.

In the 18th century BC, the Babylonian Empire became more important. And here is where we find the famous Hammurabi (Paleo-Babylonian king of Babylon).

Now, the Hittites, from the kingdom of Hatti, came from the Anatolian region, which is modern-day Turkey. At the same time, the Hurrians, from the kingdom of Mitanni, a people also from the Anatolian region, founded the Mitanni Empire. Contemporaneously, the Kassites settled in Babylon. The Kassites were a people from the mountain of Iran. It is here that the Babylonian Empire resurfaces.

The Middle Assyrian Empire conquers Mitanni and causes its extinction, and thus begins the battle again against Babylon in the south.

After the Middle Assyrian Empire and the wars with Babylon, around 1200 BC, the Invasion of the

Sea Peoples arrives in Mesopotamia. This invasion causes political disorganization. After this political disorganization, with the invasion of the Sea Peoples, the Assyrian people resurface, also known as the Neo-Assyrian Empire, around the 9th and 8th centuries BC. In the 7th century BC, the invasion of another people, the Indo-Iranians, occurs, with Babylon resurging as a result, and the whole story ends with the invasion of the Persians.

Myths of Heroes and Demons

Here, we can find several events, such as the feats of the hero Gilgamesh, as well as the first reference to vampirism in all of history: Lilith, a vampire woman who, according to Hebrew mythology, was the first wife of Adam. Lilith left paradise and became a demon to create a lineage of vampires. Are we facing the true origin of vampirism?

The myth of Gilgamesh, Enkidu, and the Netherworld

This myth found on the Sumerian tablets, tells us about a battle that Enki, lord of the waters, had against a powerful primordial monster. It also tells us about the creation of life and some important objects that emitted a powerful sound but fell into the underworld. Gilgamesh and Enkidu wanted to recover those objects.

Before analyzing this myth, you should know that Enki is not Enkidu. Enkidu means *made by Enki*. Enkidu would be a kind of hominid created to kill Gilgamesh, but Enkidu could not kill Gilgamesh, and they became friends. The Epic of Gilgamesh also mentions the feats of Enkidu and Gilgamesh. In summary, both characters want to recover those objects from the underworld.

Let's start analyzing the first fragment of text on

this tablet:

"An took the sky, Enlil took the earth, and Ereshkigal was taken to the underworld as her prey."

Ereshkigal is the name of an Anunnaki goddess who was kidnapped by the demon Kur. This demon had the appearance of a snake and lived in the primordial waters. These waters are obviously the underworld. Enki fought against Kur when the Anunnaki god went down to the underworld to rescue the goddess Ereshkigal. Enki won that fight. It is important to know that in Sumerian mythology, there is a sky, an underworld, and a super sky. The super sky is above the sky, and this is where the Anunnaki gods are living. It is interesting to see how reference is made to the Catholic concept of hell; it is an interesting coincidence. Let's keep reading the Sumerian texts:

"The tree grew slowly, but no foliage grew from its trunk because from the roots, the snake that did not know the spell made its nest there. Inside the tree, the woman Lilith built her home, and Inanna cried rivers at that moment!"

For a moment, I thought Lilith had no connections with the Sumerians, but I was wrong. Lilith is a female demon, a succubus, a being that feeds on our sexual energy while we sleep. The Sumerian legend, not the Hebrew one (the Hebrew legend is much more modern), gave Lilith the name of the first wife of Adam. Likewise, the name Lilith also refers to and is linked to other names such as the night spirit, the enemy of childbirth, and newborns.

According to legend, Lilith left Eden by her own decision and went to live by the Red Sea, where she joined Samael. Samael eventually became her lover, and then Lilith also had more lovers. These new lovers were other demons. Lilith became a demon who kidnapped children from their cribs at night and also had sexual relations with men while they slept. Lilith is a succubus demon that appears in men's dreams while they sleep. Lilith, the succubus demon, sexually abused men, thus engendering the children of Lilith, called Lilin. The Lilin, according to Hebrew mythology, are the first vampires, the ancient vampires.

It is inevitable to be surprised when finding the name Lilith in Sumerian tablets. Let's remember that Sumerian texts are the oldest texts in history, so the origin of vampirism can be found in Sumerian tablets. It wouldn't be a coincidence that the Hebrews took some notes from the Sumerian tablets. I say this because the Hebrews also narrate the Great Flood exactly like the Sumerians.

Let's continue with our analysis:

"From the roots, Gilgamesh the hero struck the great serpent that could conjure unknown spells. In its golden cup, the horrible bird Imdugud carried its offspring as it fled to the interior of the mountain. There, it encountered the beautiful Lilith, whose home it destroyed before fleeing to the desert."

This text refers to Lilith's escape from paradise. According to Hebrew mythology, Lilith left paradise, while Sumerian mythology states that she fled to the desert. Both mythologies talk about the same thing! The exile of Lilith, the serpent who left paradise!

You should know, reader, that Lilith is Ishtar (the goddess of the Sumerians), Lilith is also Inanna (the goddess of the Akkadians). Time changed her name, but not her actions or the events that link her to these mythologies. These three divinities are different names for the same deity.

We must take a step back in the previous chapters and talk about the myth of Inanna and Shukallituda. This myth tells us that Inanna fell asleep while Shukallituda sexually abused her.

Now, knowing that Inanna is Lilith, the story takes another direction as succubi absorb the sexual energy of their victims when they sleep and are submerged in the deepest dreams. Everything seems to make sense when we mix the elements: Inanna (Lilith) sleeping, creating a dream for Shukallituda to see her sleeping in the garden, he cannot help but sexually abuse her. In that sexual abuse, in that rape, there is a dream, and in that dream, there is sexual desire, and this sexual desire is a kind of energy like the one succubi use to feed on.

I don't think Lilith was raped, but rather taking advantage of the mortal Shukallituda, because it doesn't make sense for a goddess to be raped. Although this is my analysis, maybe you have another one, reader. But really, if we understand it this way, everything makes more sense.

From that moment on, vampirism became

intertwined with ancient cultures, but the oldest known references to vampires are found in Sumerian texts. This is particularly interesting because the concept of the vampire has existed since time immemorial.

If you are interested in learning more about vampires, I recommend reading books on Hebrew mythology. However, it's important to note that most of what you will find there is modern. The oldest texts on the subject come from Sumerian literature.

Let's continue reading what the tablets tell us:

"He tried to put his feet in, but they wouldn't fit. So he decided to sit in front of the enormous gate of Gaznir, the Great Horrible Eye of the Underworld. If you wish to venture into the deep underworld, listen carefully to my words: 'Do not carry a staff in your hand, lest the shadows stir before you...'

Two things are worth noting here: Gaznir is considered the main dwelling of the Underworld, or Hell, and appears in many myths. It is also the great gate that leads to the underworld's main hall.

The staff mentioned in the text refers to the dead; the Sumerians called them the Elimmu. According to their beliefs, the Elimmu were thought energy that remained on Earth after a person died because they believed the soul and spirit were connected to the mind and thought. It's important to remember that Sumerians believed in creation through the spoken word.

The next text reads:

"'Go ahead! You can open the gate of the Underworld! Release the infernal spirits, the spirit of the great and powerful Enkidu!' Someone opened the gate of Hell. 'I ask you, what did you just see?' 'I will tell you, my dear friend. I will tell you...'"

Enkidu descended into the underworld because two objects that emitted sounds had fallen into it. Unfortunately, the meaning of these sounds remains a mystery to this day, as neither I nor Federico Lara Peinado have been able to decipher them. We will never know what Enkidu saw in the underworld because the relevant parts of the tablets were destroyed and cannot be read.

Gilgamesh and Agga of Kish

These tablets tell us another myth about Gilgamesh, which was rescued from 11 tablets found in the city of Nippur dating back to 2700 years before Christ.

The translation of these tablets tells the story of the legendary hero named Gilgamesh, whose DNA was made up of 40% human blood and 60% gods blood. Commander Agga, from the city of Kish, sent an army to capture Gilgamesh and destroy Uruk, the city that Gilgamesh defended.

At the end of the myth, Gilgamesh was able to convince the invading army not to spill blood on sacred land. One very interesting text fragment reads as follows:

"Those whom King Emmebaraggesi sent, along with his

firstborn Agga, departed from Kish to confront the mighty Gilgamesh in Uruk."

According to the Sumerian king list, Agga was the last king of Kish, reigning for 625 years after the Universal Flood cataclysm. This is important because Sumerian heroes possessed god blood and lived six times longer than a normal human being. 625 years is a long time to rule. Emmebaraggesi, Agga's father, according to Sumerian tablets, reigned for more than 900 years. This proves that these kings and heroes had longer lives than human beings.

The Anunnaki gods were immortal, but the heroes and kings had a long life because they had 60% or more Anunnaki DNA. These kings and heroes had Anunnaki blood in their DNA to live healthy and prolonged lives over time. However, kings and heroes were mortal, and they would eventually die.

Now let's analyze the following text:

"Uruk, work of the gods, Eanna, the house that descends from the heavens, it has been the powerful gods who constructed its parts, for its great wall that reaches the clouds, for its beautiful home founded by Anu..."

Eanna was a temple built for the goddess Inanna. To me, this text speaks of a truly important construction, one created by the Anunnaki gods and descending from the heavens. It is possible that Eanna was an immense structure in the sky that descended to earth. This makes me think that it was a type of flying machine that descended to Earth, similar to the Vimanas of Indian culture that we have previously discussed.

Gilgamesh and the Land of the Queen Life

This myth tells the story of Gilgamesh and his friend Enkidu, who embark on a great struggle against the powerful guardian Humbaba. Humbaba was a fierce protector of the Cedar Forest, where the gods resided, and he prevented anyone from accessing their realm. In a fragment of the text, Gilgamesh says to Enkidu as they set off towards the Land of the Queen Life, which is believed to be the dwelling place of the gods:

"Oh mighty Enkidu, the great brick and the mortal seal still do not bring us mortal destiny."

There is some debate among scholars about the location of the Land of the Queen Life. Samuel Noah Kramer suggests that it may be in the Bahrain Islands, where Dilmun, the dwelling of the gods, was thought to be located. In the text, the word "courage" is mentioned, which refers to the warrior spirit that overcomes fear of death. Although the Sumerians believed that the spirit was a substance that became corporeal upon leaving the body, the gods used words and thoughts to create and destroy through the Tablets of Destiny.

Continuing with the text, Gilgamesh implores the god Utu for help in his quest for immortality, saying:

"Oh mighty god Utu, I would like to say a word to you, listen to my weak voice: In our city, men perish with burdened hearts. Men perish, their hearts no longer possess hope. I have

seen on the great wall and I have seen their corpses floating in the river. And I know that my destiny will be to perish like my brothers because the most powerful of men cannot touch the heavens with his hands."

This passage illustrates Gilgamesh's desire for immortality and his willingness to do whatever it takes to achieve it. He wants to enter the Land of the Queen Life, defeat Humbaba, and steal the plant that grants immortality. However, the gods are immortal and beyond the reach of mortal men like Gilgamesh.

Finally, the text describes seven heroes who are the offspring of the same mother.

"The first hero is a voracious lion that devours everything in its path; the second hero is a terrible serpent that kills every living being; the third hero is a voracious dragon that devours its enemies and prey without mercy; the fourth hero is fire that burns everything; the fifth hero is a terrifying winged snake that freezes hearts with fear; the sixth hero is a deadly flood that destroys and drowns nations; the seventh hero is a swift thunderbolt that cannot turn back to look behind itself."

Two important things to highlight here:

1. The Powerful Seven Heroes: These heroes were not people, but seven demons who made the earth explode from the immense skies. This attack from these demons seems to be meteorites, or perhaps missiles launched from the skies by some spacecraft of these gods?

2. In the text, we can see that dragons, serpents, and snakes are frequently mentioned. Federico Lara Peinado suggests that snakes appear in all cultures and

religions of the world. For him, it is as if all the cultures of the world had acquired the knowledge of the Sumerians. However, it is more likely that these gods are truly present in all cultures of the world. It is strange that almost all religions in the world feature snakes, dragons, and serpents. We must be objective in interpreting all of this and acknowledge that these coincidences cannot be denied. There is an influence of the reptilian gods in all of these ancient religions and cultures.

Let's continue reading the text:

"Gilgamesh said again, 'By Ninsun, who is my mother, and by Lugulbanda, who is my stepfather, I swear that I will not rest until I have killed this human, Humbaba. Whether he is a human or a powerful god, I will not stop until I reach the Land of the Living. I will bring his head to the city.' Enkidu spoke to his friend, the brave Gilgamesh: 'But I have seen him, my friend, and I tremble at the sound of his name. The fangs of that beast are like those of a sky dragon, his face is the face of the bravest lion, and no one can escape his powerful forehead that knocks down trees and reeds.'"

Humbaba is a being created by the god Utu. According to the tablets, Humbaba has a human form, but he looks very much like a dragon or serpent. He is very tall, and his strength is colossal. Gilgamesh defeats him by cutting off his head and bringing it before Enki.

The end of this story cannot be read due to the poor condition of the tablets, but we can deduce the ending from the following myth.

The Death of Humbaba, Guardian of the Cedar Forest

This tablet was found in the ancient city of Larsa, and the myth on this tablet is closely related to the previous one: *Gilgamesh and the Land of the Queen Life*. Let's read the following text:

"Humbaba let out his threatening and horrible cry against Gilgamesh, Enkidu, and their companions. At the same time, more than 50 inhabitants, colleagues of Gilgamesh, went and cut his sharp branches, then tied them and threw them near the slopes of an immense mountain, and Humbaba continued with his threatening cries."

According to Federico Lara Peinado, the horrible and threatening cries were meant to defend himself and intimidate his opponents, but a kind of spell prevented Humbaba's cries from affecting Gilgamesh, Enkidu, and the 50 inhabitants.

"At the instant the seventh cry of Humbaba ended, Gilgamesh went to Humbaba's dwelling. Humbaba's face was like that of a horrible serpent from the skies."

Humbaba was a humanoid being, but when someone approached him, they could see his true reptilian appearance, his snake-like aspect. He was an abomination, a monstrous creation. Let's continue analyzing the text:

"The warrior heart of the mighty Gilgamesh, son of the powerful Ninsun, was moved. Enkidu interceded and said: 'Whoever has never seen the destructive hands of a warrior? A

revered warrior return to Gipar.'"

This text tells us how Gilgamesh, after defeating Humbaba, has compassion for him and does not want to end his life, but Enkidu makes him reflect on killing the monstrous Humbaba. If Gilgamesh killed him, he and Enkidu could enter the Land of the Queen Life. Enkidu cut off Humbaba's head.

The text mentions the word Gipar, which means the Black Chamber that was in the temples. Gipar was a chamber where a god or the gods rested at night when they descended to Earth.

Let's continue analyzing the following text:

"'Let him sit before you, let him eat the bread that all of you eat, and also let him drink everything that you drink, after the god Enki has removed his sweet and horrible cry from his place.'"

This text mentions how, after Gilgamesh's victory and taking Humbaba's head to Enki, Enki regains Humbaba's body. Enki extracts the horrible cry from Humbaba and stores it in some container. Enki obtained Humbaba's most powerful weapon: his horrible cry.

Enki links the soul of the monster Humbaba to the lives of Enkidu and Gilgamesh by casting a curse upon them with his terrible presence.

It is interesting that they use that breath, that horrendous cry, as a weapon. I find it very interesting that Enki does something like that.

The Death of Gilgamesh

Let's read the text on this last tablet:

"Do not grieve, do not be discouraged. Who among all men made the worst mistake?"

This text tells us the despair and suffering of Gilgamesh when a snake stole the plant of immortality from him. The biblical Noah, better known to the Sumerians as Ziusudra, gave this plant to Gilgamesh. Ziusudra left this plant underwater, but the plant that Gilgamesh found underwater was stolen by a snake, and that snake could be an Anunnaki god.

Let's continue reading the following text, which, to me, is one of the most important along with the myth of Lilith:

"For the Anunnaki gods of the kingdom called Dukug, and for the small Igigi of the kingdom of Dukug."

An (Anu for the Akkadians) created the Anunnaki. These Anunnaki lived in the kingdom of Dukug, which was located east of the world. The Igigi are another creation, another race distinct from the Anunnaki. An is not an Anunnaki, he is above them. An is the creator of the Anunnaki. This makes me reflect that An has the aspect of a serpent. The Anunnaki have a serpent-like appearance due to An's genes, but their creation, the Anunnaki gods, have a human form.

So we can appreciate many differences between the beings in Sumerian culture. The Anunnaki, the Usumgal, and the Igigi are three distinct races. Don't get confused.

We will talk about these Igigi beings, as they are very similar to those gray beings, those grey aliens. But the creator of everything, An, seems to be a very different being from all the beings he created. His appearance is very different. It can then be asserted that An is another as-yet-unknown race.

The Myth of the Afterlife

For the Sumerians, there was a hell in the depths of the Earth, a hidden world protected by a guardian and seven enormous gates with seven enormous locks. Ereshkigal was the queen of the underworld and darkness. In this chapter, we will talk about this and also about life after death. For the Sumerians, there were very specific funeral rituals to elevate the Zi, which means the soul, the spirit of the dead gods. With this, the souls of the gods could wander in an immaterial world for all eternity. Let's analyze more deeply what the Sumerians thought about hell and life after death, which we will see in the tablets corresponding to the myths of the Sumerian Afterlife.

The Descent of Inanna to the Underworld.

This myth appears on 13 clay tablets that were found in the city of Nippur. These tablets are about 4,000 to 4,200 years old. The myth narrates the descent of Inanna to the underworld, the death of Inanna, and the resurrection of Inanna thanks to the intervention of Enki who resurrected her with magical brews.

These 13 tablets tell us how the husband of Inanna, Dumuzi, was seized and substituted her in death so that Inanna could escape the rules of the Sumerian underworld and return to the world of the living.

The goddess Ereshkigal, queen of the underworld and darkness, was responsible for maintaining and enforcing the rules of her realm.

Let's read the following text:

"To descend from the countless heights to the deepest of abysses, she employed her thoughts."

The countless heights refer to the heavens. The Sumerians divided the heavens into several layers, several levels. This is very similar to the atmospheric layers we know today. So it is possible that the Sumerians were aware that the sky was not the limit. They knew that there were more heavens. In other words, were they aware that there were more atmospheric layers?

When the Sumerians spoke of the deep abysses, they referred to an underground world, a world hidden beneath the earth. They linked these abysses with something dark and evil, which is consistent with the idea we have of the biblical Hell.

Let's continue analyzing the following text:

"My noble lady will abandon the heavens, abandon the beautiful earth, because she has decided to go to the terrible underworld."

When the Sumerians spoke of the underworld, we must know that this is something that was translated by scholars and translators, as this world bears a tremendous resemblance to the biblical Hell. The underworld where Inanna descends is called Kur-nu-gia in Sumerian, while the Akkadians called the underworld Erset La Tari (which means land of no return). If a mortal or god wanted to access this world, they had to enter through a huge abyss or gate. Later, we will see why there were seven gates; these seven gates were the only entrance to the abyss where the Sumerian underworlds were located.

Let's keep reading:

"Then she left Eanna to be able to descend to the terrible underworlds."

Eanna was Inanna's home, a sort of palace or floating mansion high up in the sky. The Sumerians believed that it was something static in the sky and in the air, and that the gods lived in flying boats that were similar to airplanes or spaceships. The similarity between these flying boats and modern technology is undeniable, and it makes me tremble with fear and feel bewildered. Let's continue analyzing Sumerian texts:

"The 7 Me tablets, he held them at his side, gathered all the Me tablets and carried them in his hand, placed the Me tablets on a surface, and arranged them."

We already know that Tablets Me mean Tablets of Destiny or Order. These Tablets Me were the most powerful artifacts in all of Sumerian and Akkadian culture. These tablets contained all the names of all existing beings. Having these tablets meant having absolute control; having these tablets meant having absolute power. For this reason, these artifacts were the most powerful in the world. The Tablets Me were also a deadly weapon.

These weapons were devices that the Anunnaki

gods held in their hands. This may be a type of engineering that the Anunnaki gods needed in order to descend into the underworld.

The following text tells us something very interesting:

"A beautiful necklace made of the finest lapis lazuli, a shiny gold ring like the sun, a breastplate attached to her chest, a mantle on her broad back, and her comrade Ninshubur descended to the underworld."

Here we can see how the Anunnaki goddess, Inanna, needs protection, a kind of armor to descend into the deep underworld, and not only does she need armor, but also mystical protection like the gold ring or the lapis lazuli necklace.

If we understand this, seeing through the eyes of the Sumerians, they understood all this technology as a kind of device that the Anunnaki gods had on their bodies, and armor to defend themselves. But although for the Anunnaki gods, a gold ring was just technology, for the Sumerians it was just a gold ring. That was the interpretation of the Sumerians for this technology of the gods. This interpretation is based on the objects they used in their daily lives.

Let's continue our reading:

"Ninshubur visited Enki, the god of wisdom. He knows what 'the food of this life' is, he knows what 'the drink of this life' is. I'm sure he will make me resurrect again."

According to Sumerian tablets, Ninshubur visited several gods, including Enki and Enlil. Enlil ignored Ninshubur's presence, but Enki listened to him. Enki told Ninshubur that if Inanna would die in the underworld, Enki would give her the food and drink of life so that she could resurrect and leave the underworld.

Ninshubur, who was in love with Inanna and her faithful servant, made a trip to ask for help from the gods, but only Enki listened to him. Enki created a type of chemical or brew known as the food and drink of life to obtain immortality. In Sumerian culture, we see that these gods and the subsequent kings, whether human or hybrid, gods or men, all lived for more than 800 years, some even exceeding 1000 or 1200 years in their dynasties. It is possible that the ancient Sumerians knew the secret of eternal youth and immortality. Let's keep reading:

"In the castle of the underworld, Inanna said, 'Open this castle, guardian! Open this castle! Open the castle, Neti, for I will enter alone!' Neti replied, 'Why have you come to the underworld?' Inanna responded, 'Because the husband of Ereshkigal has been killed.' Inanna entered the castle of Lady Ereshkigal, and Ereshkigal said to Inanna, 'Oh, my lady, you are a maiden and come without anyone to accompany you, with that appearance of divinity, you are at the gate.' Ereshkigal said to Neti, 'Open the great gate of the underworld, remove the seven enormous bolts, the all-seeing eye in the underworld. Open the door of the castle, and when she has entered, ashamed and without clothing, bring her to me.' When the goddess Inanna entered, her golden crown, beautiful necklace of fine lapis lazuli, golden ring, and the pectoral of her chest were removed because the laws of the underworld are all perfect."

In hell there were guardians, Neti was one of them. Neti protected the 7 gates and their 7 locks. Samuel Noah Kramer and Federico Lara Peinado disagreed on whether the gate of the underworld had 7 locks, or if these 7 locks belonged to each of these 7 gates.

Ereshkigal is the Anunnaki goddess of the underworld and darkness, she was the sister of Inanna and other Anunnaki gods.

The text also tells us about the Eye of the Underworld, and here there is much controversy. None of the translators and academics really know what the Eye of the Underworld, which watches the gates, means. It is still unknown today what the Sumerians referred to when they spoke of the Eye of the Underworld. There is no further information on this Eye of the Underworld.

Some scholars believe that the Eye of the Underworld was a kind of mechanism that judged those who wanted to enter the world of the underworld. But again, the Eye of the Underworld is truly unknown to translators and academics.

When Inanna is spoken of as being naked and ashamed, it is the same as her being humiliated as she passed through the seven gates, losing her objects one by one. These objects protected Inanna, and when they were taken away, she was left naked in the underworld, a world that had different rules from the world of the heavens.

In hell, everyone had to follow the rules. In this infernal world, there may have been a kind of mechanism that forced visitors to comply and obey these rules. Let's keep reading the texts:

"Ereshkigal observed Inanna from the tip of her toes to above her head. In Ereshkigal's gaze, there was death. After saying something to Inanna, Inanna began to fall ill, and her body became that of a corpse, which was hung on a nail. Following three dismal days and three horrible nights, her companion Ninshubur went to Enlil for help. Enlil said, 'Inanna, my heir, has been very ambitious,' and did not listen to Ninshubur anymore. Ninshubur then went to Enki, and Enki said, 'What happened to my offspring? I will save her.' He removed some dirt from his fingernails and created a Kurgarru and a Kalaturru. He gave the Kurgarru the food of life and the Kalaturru the drink of life, and he wet Inanna with the drink of life. Inanna stood up on her two feet. 'If Inanna wants to leave the underworld, give us someone who will die for her,' said Ereshkigal."

Kurgarru and Kalaturru, according to Federico Lara Peinado, were asexual beings. They were artificial beings created by Enki. It is fascinating to know how Enki can grant and take away life on some occasions. We can also see that Hell is mentioned. Hell or Underworld has its rules, and no one can ever leave Hell once they enter it, unless there is someone who will substitute for whoever dared to enter the underworld. This was what Inanna intended to do to be able to leave Hell, as she had died and then, with the help of Enki, was able to resurrect.

It is also incredible to see how Ereshkigal was able to kill a god, even turning her into a putrefied corpse just by using words.

Let's continue analyzing the texts:

"The cruel tiny demons gallu seized Inanna. These demons did not eat or drink; they stole the wife from the arms of her husband and took the baby from her bosom. The goddess Inanna left the underworld. Dumuzi, the guide, took Inanna's hands, and Dumuzi turned pale."

The gallu were demons who lived in the underworld, and they all carried spears. These gallu demons remind us of those demons that appeared in Dante Alighieri's Inferno or in Christian culture. These demons also appear in Sumerian tablets, and they are the ones who accompany Inanna out of Hell to find a substitute and put him in Hell. Outside of Hell, these demons find Dumuzi, Inanna's husband. Dumuzi is frightened and turns pale when arrested by these gallu demons.

Dumuzi lives in Hell and exchanges his place with his sister Geshtinanna every six months. Dumuzi became Inanna's husband, which is something I don't understand. How is it possible for Inanna to abandon her husband Dumuzi like that? There are some explanations in the Sumerian tablets that may better explain all this.

Now, Dumuzi exchanging his stay in Hell with his sister Geshtinanna means that this is a metaphor for the change of harvest. The change of harvest is the harvest of a particular food according to each season of the year since Dumuzi is the god of the field and agriculture.

The Death of Dumuzi

These tablets narrate to us how the death of Dumuzi occurred. This myth does not speak of Inanna's descent to the underworld, but it is intimately linked to it.

Basically, this myth tells us how Dumuzi was arrested by these gallu demons and also narrates how Dumuzi manages to escape from the underworld on three occasions, since the god Utu grants him salvation.

I remember that the tablets also narrated how Dumuzi transformed into animals; that is, the god Dumuzi changed his appearance into several animals to be able to escape from the underworld. However, in the last escape, five gallu demons kill Dumuzi, and on this occasion, he dies, not returning to the underworld or the world of the living, but dies according to this myth written on these Sumerian tablets. I have not selected any specific texts from the tablets, as they are very short. This is basically a summary of the tablets.

Inanna and Bilulu

This myth is written on a broken tablet, found in the Sumerian city of Nippur, and it tells an alternative story of the death of Dumuzi. That is, Bilulu murders Dumuzi and Inanna mourns the death of her husband Dumuzi. When Inanna confronts Bilulu, Bilulu turns her and her son, Girgire, into an Utuku and a Lama, respectively.

The Utuku and the Lama were demons very similar to the Gallu, with some differences. It is also said in Sumerian texts that there were 7 demons who were once gods and that for some unknown event, they were cursed.

The Passion of Lil in the Tomb

This tablet tells us about the close relationship that the Sumerians had with the underworld. It also talks about their understanding of life and death, and its contents place us in the Sumerian myth of The Death of the God Lil and the concern of his sister, Ekime, goddess of secrets, for her brother's irreversible death.

At one point, in the myth written on this tablet, the spirit of the god Lil is released and wanders in an immaterial and eternal form in our plane, in our world.

Here we can see that in the oldest culture of all (the Sumerian culture), these spirits and ghosts exist, something that for the belief of many people today is true, is real. People of our time believe that there are fictional ghosts and spirits that wander the world. Even horror movies portray these fictional ghosts and spirits.

It's amazing to see how the Sumerians already spoke and knew about the spirit world. It is possible that the Sumerians had more secrets and knowledge of how to access the place where the cursed spirits of the gods wander eternally. Let's analyze the following text:

"May my lady mother, who fears for my life, extend the

Silah."

The Silah is a funeral ritual that specifically served to release the spirit of a god, of a spirit, in this case, Lil's spirit. This ritual makes Lil's spirit wander in a material plane, as a material entity.

The Creation of Everything

In this chapter, I have gathered all the Sumerian tablets about the Enuma Elish myth, the Creation of Everything. The translation is faithful to that of the best translators who have studied these tablets for over 30 years. Here, Nudimmud (known as Enki to the Sumerians and Ea to the Akkadians) is an important character.

Tablet 1

When in the heights nothing yet had a name, when in the vastness of space there was absolutely nothing, much less the then dark skies or the dustiest of lands...

And so it was that from the most incalculable heights, the primordial and powerful gods, Abzu and Tiamat, mixed in a magical broth the waters that belonged to both of them to create the first gods, their first offspring.

From that magical mixture appeared two gods, who were the greatest and most fearsome serpent beings that any eye had ever seen. The names of these gods, the names of these offspring were almost unpronounceable, they were the god Lahmu and the goddess Lahamu.

Before the new gods, Lahmu and Lahamu, grew up and became almighty, they begot two more offspring: Anshar, the protective deity and owner of the sky, and Kishar, the goddess and owner of the already existing earth. These two new offspring were superior and more powerful than their parents.

These last two offspring gods created another god, whose name was, as far as is known, An (that is, Anu), his destiny was to see in eternity how things would change impressively. The firstborn offspring of this god, An, was called by him Nudimmud (better known as Ea or Enki). This god was born with the gift of knowledge and was the wisest of all the wise. His power was incalculable, no one could fight against his power.

When in the heights there were already many gods, they all went to live in the bowels of the maternal and primordial deity of everything that existed, the maternal deity Tiamat.

When they all lived inside Tiamat, the maternal goddess of everything could not rest because they disturbed the silence that resided there. In the vast heavens, the noises were tremendous and she could not be at peace. But Tiamat was able to forget her anger because she was the maternal goddess of all the gods, and there was always forgiveness in her generous heart. However, Abzu, her husband and the father of the gods, was insane and was tremendously annoyed with the children he had created. His children made noise in the sky and he could not allow such audacity.

Mummu, the Messenger of the gods, was summoned by Abzu to plan a solution to the disorder that his children were creating. Abzu wanted to speak with his wife, the maternal deity Tiamat.

Both parents fought because Abzu, the father of everything, wanted to make all his offspring disappear from existence, but the mother of everything, Tiamat, with her kind motherly heart, preferred not to punish them with Abzu's curse. She said to him, 'Abzu, why do you want to make our beloved children disappear? Let us be wise and understand, let us have hope in them.'

After speaking with his beloved Tiamat, Abzu heard Mummu's recommendation. Mummu recommended that Abzu ignore his dear wife and destroy all the creation that he and Tiamat had conceived, so that they could regain the peace they had once known.

Abzu agreed to destroy all his children. The divine creations heard the entire conversation between Abzu and Mummu and felt terror, felt great fear at the thought of disappearing from existence.

But Mummu and Abzu did not expect something. Nudimmud (that is, Ea, Enki), the god of knowledge, the divine being with absolute wisdom among all his brothers the gods. Nudimmud created a wonderful and complex plan to be able to rid himself of Abzu's fury, the primordial deity.

Through a powerful and complicated spell, Nudimmud caused Abzu to fall into the deepest of sleeps from which he could never awaken.

Nudimmud removed the shining golden crown from the head of Mummu, the Messenger of the gods, stripped him of his glowing aura, and chained him up.

Nudimmud then adorned himself with Mummu's glowing aura and used the immeasurable body of the father of everything, the primordial deity Abzu, to create his own kingdom. Within Abzu, Nudimmud married the goddess Ninhursag, and from this union, the new god Marduk was born.

When An (Anu) met his grandson Marduk, he knew that the future of his grandson would be to become the most powerful of all deities, for Marduk had the necessary qualities to achieve this. When Marduk spoke, fire from the sun could be seen in his mouth. His face had two pairs of ears and two pairs of eyes, which enabled him to see far into the immortal universe.

For An, Marduk would be the most powerful of all his children and siblings. An also saw that Marduk possessed 10 powerful auras and 50 terrible flashes of lightning within his tiny body, flashes of lights as powerful as thunders.

An was overjoyed at the birth of his little grandson and created the four terrible and deadly winds. An gave the four winds to Marduk as a gift to play with on earth so that he would not get bored.

However, every disaster caused by Marduk stirred up terrible storms of dust and sand, which greatly angered the maternal goddess Tiamat and her children, the other deities.

The children of the maternal goddess Tiamat protested. They could not understand why she allowed the death of Abzu, her husband, and why An and his descendants did as they pleased, especially Marduk, who played with the four terrible and deadly winds, destroying everything on earth. The children of the maternal goddess Tiamat could not understand why Tiamat did not punish the descendants of An. They demanded revenge and justice

Half of Tiamat's children forced her to destroy An and his descendants for the crimes they had committed, because there was no peace in the high heavens. Half of Tiamat's children needed to rest as they did before the creation of An.

Tiamat obeyed this request, and with a huge army of warriors, she prepared to declare war on An and his descendants. She took the water from the infernal world of Kubur, with which all things were created, and used it as a *weapon of creation. She created thousands of horrible and terrible dragons, sharp weapons, many gigantic and horrible leviathans, immortal hydras, predatory dogs and lions, men with scorpion bodies, humanoid fish, and many more monstrosities that possessed formidable weaponry.*

Among these beasts were 11 beasts that were the most powerful. Tiamat chose her most faithful vassal, Kingu, as the leader of her troops, whom she named as the twelfth beast. Kingu was the most powerful and a natural leader. Then Tiamat said to Kingu, "I have granted you all my power in magic and sorcery, go and show that you are the best of all the Anunnaku of my descendants."

Tiamat gave Kingu the Tablet of Destiny, the Me Tablet, the most destructive and devastating artifact of all that existed at that time.

This war would begin when the maternal deity Tiamat made her voice heard throughout the universe. She would shout and her fury would fall upon the descendants of An.

Tablet 2

Tiamat was ready to begin the destruction of the descendants of An. Her great army was powerful; but Nudimmud (also known as Ea, Enki), the god of knowledge and wisdom, reflected on how to combat this Apocalypse that would be unleashed upon him and the descendants of An.

The 11 groups that belonged to Tiamat's army were led by Kingu, who was the leader of this enterprise. In Kingu's chest was the most powerful artifact in the universe: the Tablet of Destinies, which could be used for creation or destruction of anything using only a word.

Anshar encouraged Nudimmud to be the mythical hero who would save his race from extinction. Nudimmud's mission would be to kill the primordial goddess Tiamat and her powerful group of beasts.

Nudimmud was the hope of his race, as his previous feat of killing the god Abzu and his colleague Mummu meant to his brothers that he would save them again.

After hearing the words of his beloved grandfather, Nudimmud was very afraid and proposed that the hero of this great and monumental war by his father, An (Anu), since he was the most powerful of all the Anunnaki. An did not flinch and accepted the challenge. To combat the terrible threat approaching the Anunnaki, An brought out the mightiest of all weapons, Kazuzu, the technological weapon of infinite power.

This weapon (Kazuzu) would be used if the goddess Tiamat did not hear his voice. Anshar, Nudimmud's grandfather, wanted to solve this misunderstanding without bloodshed, but he hid the Kazuzu in case he ever needed it.

An tried to talk to the goddess Tiamat, but when An saw all the monstrosities she had created he decided to run away.

When Anshar learned of his son An's failure, he became very frightened and decided to gather all his Anunnaki children and their allies (the Igigi) in an assembly to discuss the near future. The Igigi were another race that together with the Anunnaki gods were the masters of the heavens.

In this assembly, many voted for Marduk to be the hero who would defeat the goddess Tiamat. The courage of the already adult Marduk and his knowledge of sorcery, inherited from his father Nudimmud, were his main characteristics to be able to defeat Tiamat.

Tablet 3

After that useful meeting, the older gods were informed. These ancient gods had more authority over all the other gods. These ancient gods were the god Lahmu and the god Lahamu, parents of the god Anshar, who, when they understood what was happening, were worried, and it was not only them but also the grays (the Igigi). But the war had already started, and there was no way to stop it.

Tablet 4

Marduk is now the king of the Anunnaki. He has occupied the throne of An, and all admire and revere him, including his parents Nudimmud and Ninhursag. Marduk had proved himself to be the king of all the Anunnaki, using the power of the word to destroy all the stars in the heavens and also to rebuild them.

An gave his grandson Marduk the weapon Kazuzu to go and fight. Marduk built for himself a great bow, a powerful mace, and several arrows. His body was covered in armor shining like the flames of the sun, and on his forehead, he carried a lightning bolt that would strike down any enemy. He also carried the gift of his grandfather An: the four terrible and deadly winds, as well as the seven winds that he created with his own hands.

He put all the winds behind his back, creating a destructive deluge, and then boarded his chariot of devastation to face Tiamat. His chariot was driven by steeds whose fangs contained poison, and he placed all the powerful winds and the rest of his weapons in the chariot.

From Marduk's helmet came powerful bursts of light, and his armor had tongues of fire like those of the sun, frightening his enemies. When he arrived before Tiamat, Marduk used a spell to counter the spell sent by Tiamat. To avoid dying from Tiamat's poisonous breath, Marduk ate a plant.

Suddenly, Kingu, the best and most powerful warrior of the goddess Tiamat, appeared, causing Marduk to tremble with terror and turn pale. Taking advantage of Marduk's distraction, Tiamat cast a terrible spell on him.

The other Anunnaki gods joined Marduk, and together they fought against all the abominations created by Tiamat. Marduk sent his mighty winds into the immeasurable mouth of the goddess Tiamat, filling her belly with all those winds and preventing her from closing her immeasurable mouth. Then he attacked her with all his spells, finally piercing her entrails with an arrow and splitting her in two.

Marduk walked towards the dead goddess Tiamat, and all the monsters she had created disappeared from his sight. All those deities who had advised Tiamat to destroy the Anunnaki feared for their lives in the face of Marduk's power.

The eleven mighty monsters could not escape and were caught in thick nets and imprisoned. Kingu tried to assassinate Marduk, but his attacks had no effect.

Marduk took the Me Tablet that Tiamat had given to Kingu, becoming the new bearer. He sealed this Tablet Me with his name. Tiamat's body was used for different purposes: the Anunnaki used the north wind to hide the red blood of this goddess, and with her disgusting skin, they created the sky of the whole universe, that is, the infinite cosmos. Two gigantic guards guarded the waters that were the body of the goddess

Tiamat.

Before giving power back to all the gods, Marduk traveled through all the hiding places of the new heavens. Then he had An, Enlil, and Nudimmud (i.e., Ea, Enki) placed in the Esh-Sarra where they would rule. The Esh-Sarra is a construction inspired by the anatomy of the Abzu.

Tablet 5

After defeating Tiamat and her monsters, Marduk decided to create a new world on Earth. He used the blue North Star in the universe, Nibiru, to create all the other constellations.

Once he had distributed these constellations, he assigned constellations to Nudimmud and Enlil.

Using the rotting corpse of the goddess Tiamat, Marduk created the Earth. He used Tiamat's saliva to create the beautiful skies, the air, and the round white clouds.

With Tiamat's huge head, he created the most gigantic of all the mountains that ever existed on Earth. In just a few days, many rivers such as the Euphrates and the Tigris flowed from the long nose of the dead goddess Tiamat.

Marduk turned the monstrous beasts spawned by Tiamat into stone and hid them all over the Earth. He then assigned the power, roles, and tasks that the gods would perform on Earth. When he finished with these tasks, he ordered his subjects to build a sanctuary for him to rest, and he gave the name Tiamat to this floating city.

The Anunnaki gods needed workers to construct their buildings, so Marduk created man and used him as a slave, ordering them to worship the gods. To create this new being, he asked for the help of his father Nudimmud, who was the wisest *and the owner of knowledge.*

Tablet 6

Nudimmud needed the blood of Kingu in order to create men. The blood of the dead warrior Kingu was mixed with the thick mud that was on Earth, and thus, men came into being.

Then, in Babylon, all the corners of the Earth knew more than 50 names of Marduk, and thus, all knew of his great power.

Tablet 7

Once the 50 names of the god Marduk were known, he was recognized as having absolute power over all existence. The best-known name of this god was Nibiru, as Marduk believed himself to be as bright and powerful as this star.

Nudimmud named his beloved son, Marduk, which was significant because many kings of antiquity named their successors after themselves when they were old or knew that their offspring would make good kings. This act of Nudimmud towards Marduk shows that he gave him absolute control to rule over all that exists. Nudimmud also gave him the Me Tablets, the Tablets of Destiny.

More Sacred Texts

Before I begin, I would like to mention that the *Enuma Elish, the Origin of Everything* that we saw in the previous chapter, does not belong to the Sumerians. Although its roots are in Sumerian culture, it was written on Babylonian tablets.

Let us remember that Sumer, Akkadia, and Babylon were different civilizations. Many civilizations took the Sumerians as their guides and teachers to start their civilizations. They changed the names of Sumerian gods, customs, and myths and incorporated this knowledge into their civilizations.

For example, Marduk was an important god for the Akkadians and Babylonians, but the Sumerians believed that Marduk was a minor god, of little relevance.

If you understand this, then you will understand that the Enuma Elish is an adaptation of Sumerian religion within the Babylonian religion.

Let's analyze the rest of the tablets.

"When the sky did not yet possess a name and the earth did not know its name."

This text tells us that something must have a name to exist. If something doesn't have a name, then it doesn't exist. This is interesting because it refers to the power of Hermeticism and the Law of Attraction.

The mind or the name is the origin of ideas. If something cannot be thought of, then it does not exist. Therefore, even the concept of nothingness exists because it can be thought of.

For the Sumerians, magic resided in the power of the mind, in the power of ideas, and in naming things. The Sumerian word 'Me' means name or guideline, a law. The Me tablets were objects used by the Anunnaki gods to make existence real.

Let's continue Reading:

"The god An begot is a god named Nudimmud, who was very similar to him. Nudimmud was a being with great wisdom, surpassing all others in intelligence, and his strength was comparable to that of An."

Nudimmud was Ea, who is also known as Enki. This concept can be difficult to grasp. However, a colleague of mine who is an expert in archeology and specializes in studying classical cultures explained it to me. In Sumerian culture, the gods were not just represented by names, but also by ideograms. This means that divinity could have different names but played the same role in all other religions. For instance, Enki was the god of the Sumerians, Ea was the god of the Akkadians, and Nudimmud was the god of the Babylonians.

Let us read on:

"The gods fought against each other and this annoyed Tiamat, their battle roars were heard in the bowels of Tiamat. In the heavens, their battles were heard."

Apparently, the Sumerians are referring to some cataclysm made by the gods themselves, it is the only explanation. There is no other. Those rumblings, those annoying noises were caused by the gods, there is no doubt.

Perhaps this great explosion, these rumblings, were not only provoked to annoy Tiamat. Perhaps all this is the collision of two great planets.

Perhaps the Enuma Elish catastrophe is a cosmic-level catastrophe.

We can also see here something very interesting: the interior of Tiamat. What do the Sumerians mean by this? Is it possible that the gods are inside Tiamat? Tiamat is a primordial goddess. So, if the gods were inside her, perhaps Tiamat was a mother ship, even a planet. Is it possible that Tiamat is a planet? Is it possible that this planet has life, and the inhabitants, i.e. the gods, are destroying it?

Let us read on:

"Nudimmud organized a plan to cast his spells against him. Nudimmud was bold, read his spells to him by employing a sieve, and cast his best spell against Abzu, who then plunged into eternal sleep."

According to Federico Lara Peinado, the sieve or filter means water. Ea used water so that his spell would have the necessary effect to put the god Abzu to sleep.

It is curious that in ancient Sumer, water is related to spells because water was the catalyst for many magicians of the seventeenth and eighteenth centuries to make their spells. Water was used as a method of control and utilization for those magical arts, those esoteric arts. Is it possible that water has even more secrets that we do not know?

Let us read on:

"When he put the primordial god Abzu to sleep, Mummu, the one who delivered the messages, did not watch over the welfare of his lord, so Nudimmud removed his robes and his golden crown. Abzu lost his divinity; Nudimmud had taken it from him."

For the Sumerians, the divinity of the gods was the aura. The aura was a divine splendor. This aura was known as Me-Lamo, and it was similar to an armor of energy that perhaps gave the wearer unlimited power and special abilities. So, this divine splendor is very important in the Babylonian myth of the Enuma Elish, the Origin of Everything.

This text also mentions that Nudimmud made Abzu sleep. In reality, Abzu did not sleep; he was dead. Then, Nudimmud used Abzu's corpse to erect his home there.

It is very striking to me that Abzu becomes something inanimate, something lifeless. Abzu was the Great Abyss. Abzu was a god who died and became the Great Abyss. Would we be talking about Abzu being a great monster, and Nudimmud, after killing it, would enter the interior of this monster and create his home there?

I don't know if Abzu is a planet or a mothership, but like Tiamat, both could be ships or planets. This is my guess after reading and analyzing Sumerian tablets.

Abzu may also be a destroyed planet or half of a

destroyed planet.

Let's continue analyzing the Sumerian texts:

"He noted the power of Marduk. 'His aura is divine, different from all others, he is unsurpassed. His shining body is marvelous, worthy of a king; his aura is unbelievably great, incalculable his power, no one could look at him for long. His precious eyes are 4, and his tiny ears, which are 4, can hear every corner of the universe'."

For the Babylonians, Marduk is the main god. The Akkadians and Babylonians had substituted the mighty An (Anu), the father of the Anunnaki, for Marduk. In doing so, the Babylonian culture had implanted the premature germ of monotheism. That is, that people were to have only one god.

This process was slow, very slow. The Babylonians slowly began to forget the other gods and worshipped only Marduk. This is how the first practice of monotheism began by the first civilizations of the world.

Federico Lara Peinado states that he finds it very curious that Marduk's physical appearance is mentioned a lot, that is, his 4 ears and 4 eyes. This is something very strange.

Let us read on:

"Marduk possesses the crown of the most powerful gods, the mighty 10 gods, he is also protected by the 50 bright lightning bolts. Anu gave his destructive creation to Marduk, the 4 terrible and deadly winds".

The crowns were placed on the heads of the gods. They were the almighty exaltation of the gods. The 50 bright lightning bolts refer to the 50 names of Marduk that later the gods and humans would bestow upon him as titles and recognition of his enormous power.

The bright lightning bolts apparently would be a kind of weapon, a technology that gave power to the gods.

What the Sumerians saw, with the little knowledge that they had at that time, if the Sumerians saw that technology (shots in the air, atomic explosions, those kinds of weapons), there is no doubt that their only explanation would be that they are lightning bolts, because the Sumerians could not understand what was going on. They didn't understand anything about that technology.

We don't really know what happened, we can only read and analyze what they wrote in the text of this tablet.

Let's continue reading:

"The mother who formed all things, Kubur, stored the most powerful weapons, dragons of immeasurable height and sharp fangs. She placed the most deadly poisons in their majestic bodies, she took their blood and placed those poisons. She gave a terrible aspect to the horrible leviathans and placed on their heads glittering crowns. These crowns were the property of the gods. She gave birth to and formed thousands of horrible and terrible dragons, also sharp weapons, many gigantic and hideous leviathans, immortal hydras, predatory dogs and lions, scorpion-bodied men, humanoid fish, and many more monstrosities possessing formidable weaponry."

The Babylonians believed that a substance formed

the gods, this substance was capable of creating things, it had the same power as mind and name. The Babylonians believed that this substance came from a river that was in hell. This substance was known to them as Kubur. The Babylonians considered this substance a goddess, the goddess Kubur.

The Sumerians speak about this substance from hell, they called it Idludu. We can appreciate here how the names change according to the cultures.

The names of the monsters have been translated indicating the aspect of these beings that were in the drawings of the tablets. Obviously, the Babylonians did not know the hydras, the dragons, I do not think they knew the scorpion-bodied men and all those mythological monsters. These monsters exist in other cultures such as the Greek culture, the Egyptian culture, and the Dogon culture, among others cultures.

Translators have tried to be as accurate as possible in describing these mythological monsters. For example, the Sumerians called the leviathans Musamakue, the dragons Ushumgallu, the angry dogs Bashmu, the scorpion-bodied men Girtablullu, and other monsters.

There is one monster: the bull-man or bison man, which for the Sumerians would be Kusarikku. There are several translators who believe that Kusarikku means bull men or bison men, but for others, it only means hairy men. There is no doubt that this monster could have been a minotaur, like the one in Greek mythology.

It is always good to read and study different translations in order to check the veracity of the texts.

Let's read on:

"She raised the mighty Kingu and bestowed upon him leadership; he would be the one to lead the brave army. The lady believed in him and bestowed upon him this great honor, and so he was able to take his place on the throne of privilege. She also bestowed upon him the Tablet of Destiny, and he fastened it to her thorax."

Kingu is the twelfth monster in Tiamat's army and would lead her great army.

These 12 monsters resemble in number the 12 signs of the zodiac and also the 12 apostles of Jesus. Is there ancient and hidden knowledge from ancient Sumer that has been modified in other cultures? It is also curious that Kingu is the chosen warrior who would fight against the Anunnaki. These Anunnaki gods, in the myth of the *Creation of Everything*, are called Anunnaku, sons of Anu (An) and Ki.

The Enuma Elish is a text, a myth, perhaps the most epic of all. This myth tells us how two armies fought: an army of monsters and another army of gods who fought in order to resolve a conflict. However, this can also be a reference to the clash of two gigantic planets.

There has been much discussion about the planet Faetón or Phaeton, translated into English. There is a possibility that the planet Mars was the satellite of this planet Phaeton, which was destroyed by a great cosmic catastrophe. The remains of Phaethon would be the Asteroid Belt that exists beyond Mars if we were to travel there.

One possibility is that the texts refer to this event, but there is also another theory that suggests the formation of the Moon and the Earth through a collision. This theory proposes that the Moon was once a much larger planet that collided with our planet, resulting in the formation of our current planet.

That is a possibility. I know. But these myths talk a lot about a great cataclysm, maybe they refer to these events.

Maybe Tiamat was the Moon and Abzu the Sun? Or maybe the Earth was the result of a huge collision with a third planet? This is what this text implies.

I must emphasize that all of these are my interpretations based on my understanding. It is possible that you may have your own interpretation as well. If we both agree on this, then it is a great possibility.

It is important to acknowledge that no one has the absolute truth, and we can only make interpretations based on translations done by the best translators in the world. These translators have dedicated half of their lives studying these tablets, and we owe the knowledge we have gained to them. As a reader, I urge you to think for yourself and draw your own conclusions.

I have provided you with translated texts directly

from the tablets. It is now your responsibility to interpret these translations as you see fit. Each person is free to interpret these translations in their own way. It is important to note that these translations have no relation to Sitchin's fictional stories.

The translations of these tablets represent what really happened according to the Sumerians, the Akkadians, and the Babylonians. As lovers of the story of the Anunnaki, we must continue to investigate and delve deeper in order to uncover the truth.

More Translated Texts

Let us now begin analyzing tablet number 2:

"'The command you have given me in the fields. The faster I did, yes. I, Abzu, at this time, eliminated those who have rebelled against me, I have destroyed them, I have torn them to pieces.' Upon hearing this, Anshar felt happy."

This fragment is very interesting as it provides insight into the reality of the tablets. Additionally, it is unfortunate that many of these tablets cannot be read due to their deteriorated state.

Let's keep reading the texts:

"Anu, here you have the destroying weapon of all those brave heroes. Anyone who owns this weapon will have no rival."

This weapon was Kazuzu, a technology that the humans of that time could not comprehend. For the Sumerians, this was a devastating and apocalyptic force that they considered to be supernatural. It is possible that Kazuzu was a nuclear bomb or a form of nuclear weaponry.

If a tribe far from our civilization were to witness the explosion of a nuclear bomb, they would likely view it as a supernatural event.

Let us read on:

"All the Igigi beings attended the great assembly and there were the Anunnaki gods."

Who were these Igigi? The Igigi were beings, a race distinct from the Anunnaki. The Igigi disagreed with the Anunnaki on many things and ideas.

The Igigi lived in the heavens as deities, as gods, just like the Anunnaki gods. They lived their lives without intervening in the lives of the Anunnaki, except when necessary.

The Bible speaks of these Igigi beings. In the Bible, the Igigi beings are called The Watchers.

What I will say is only my interpretation. Don't worry. According to the Sumerian tablets, the Igigi also have a history. The Sumerians describe the appearance of these Igigi beings and remind us of those alien beings called the Grey Aliens. The Sumerian tablets describe them as having large eyes. The eyes of the Grey Aliens, the Greys, were huge. But that's just my interpretation. Don't worry about it.

Let us continue reading tablet 3:

"'Oh my god rescue those who have put their faith in you; but put to death the god who has created all evil.' When he put in the midst of them all the brightest constellation in the universe, he could create and destroy the constellation using the word."

Once again, we see the importance of the word in building or destroying reality. The Me Tablets or Tablets of Destiny channeled all the power of destruction and creation. The constellations were the gods, and as we recall from an earlier text, Marduk was destroying a constellation to create a new one. Marduk's plan was to consolidate himself as a god in the Celestial Vault, where all the gods resided. In other words, Marduk wanted to be part of the constellations in the universe.

Let us continue reading tablet 4:

"'And so it is that my mighty lord created the terrible flood, the mightiest weapon he possessed and got into his glittering chariot, which was drawn by vigorous steeds and carried his destroying winds to attack his enemies.'"

That mighty lord is undoubtedly Marduk, who was already considered all-powerful. In the text fragment, there is a reference to the Great Flood, which we have discussed before. It is worth noting that the Flood appears not only in the Bible but also in more than 200 stories and myths of cultures and civilizations around the world, many of which are older than the Bible.

Thus, we have irrefutable proof that the Flood existed before the Bible.

The text tells us about chariots and steeds. These chariots and steeds mean that the Sumerians wanted to represent Marduk's transport ship. They wanted to describe the flying ship in which the god Marduk traveled.

When the Sumerians wrote these tablets, the only transportation vehicle they knew of were chariots. Chariots were vehicles pulled by steeds. That is why they decided to represent that flying ship as a chariot. I hope you have understood this.

Let's read on:

"The goddess Tiamat tried to swallow him by opening her monstrous mouth, but Marduk was able to stuff his mighty

winds into her belly preventing her from closing her lips."

Marduk filled Tiamat's belly with his winds to prevent her from casting any harmful spells against him. Tiamat is a being as immense as a planet. Tiamat could eat the Anunnaki in one bite. And those winds that enter Tiamat destroy its interior. Those winds remind me of the *Star Wars* movie where Luke Skywalker fires missiles into the Death Star and destroys it. What if the Sumerians saw something like that? Obviously, they didn't understand that technology, so those missiles or lightning or destructions, made by this advanced technology of the gods, were called by the Sumerians winds or storms. But that's just my interpretation. I said there was a possibility that Tiamat is a planet with a life of its own, or maybe a mothership as big as a planet. Maybe Tiamat is a huge ship like the Death Star from *Star Wars*; however, I repeat, this is just my imagination and interpretation.

What matters here are the translations of the tablets. It is your duty to find out and investigate more about this. You must give it meaning and interpret it for yourself. You must find your own truth.

But finally, I have come to believe that this is just the collision between two planets: Tiamat colliding with Phaethon, and Phaethon could be the god Marduk. But we will analyze this in the following chapters. Let us continue reading the texts of the tablets:

"And with cruel mallet he split his great skull, then severed

the channels through which his blood was draining, the channels being carried away by the mighty wind from the north. Laying down his head, Marduk saw with pleasure the dead body of Tiamat. He severed her disgusting skin and created precious things with it."

This text tells us about the remains of Tiamat. Marduk saw something of great value in the remains of Tiamat, so he decided to hide it using the powerful north wind and hiding it in secret places.

The disgusting skin used to create precious things, according to Federico Lara Peinado, would be Ivana-niclati. Ivana-niclati would be the substance of this world (i.e., Tiamat) used to create our universe and all matter. For Federico Lara Peinado, this is a metaphor to affirm that the remains of Tiamat created reality, the cosmos, and later the time of men on Earth.

It is curious that this text tells us that after the destruction, life appears, a new world, a new dawn.

"The god Marduk flew through the new heavens and checked all the hiding places that existed. Then he sent his father Ea, his uncle Enlil, and his grandfather An to live in the sanctuary of Esharra."

Flying through the skies was a very important task for Marduk because the cosmos was created – something new and immense. Marduk had to discover and visit all these places to obtain the information needed by the ruler and chief of all the Anunnaki. That is, Marduk was the governor and chief of all the Anunnaki. He traveled the new universe to gather all the information about these new places.

The Esharra is a house, a huge sanctuary that floated in the sky and was created in the image and likeness of the corpse of Abzu. Abzu was killed by Ea (i.e., Nudimmud, Enki). Ea was the father of Marduk.

In this palace, the Trinity of the most important gods: Ea (Enki), An (Anu), and Enlil could be found. When these three gods began to live in the Esharra sanctuary, that is when the story of the Anunnaki that we know began. The history of the Anunnaki is written in the Sumerian tablets 5, 6, and 7, which we will see in the next chapter.

After the death of Tiamat, when the war between the Anunnaki and Tiamat's army ended, many events occurred that deserve to be analyzed. This book contains all of these events on its pages because we are reliving the forgotten history of the human race.

It has taken me a long time to compile this collection of Sumerian tablets, translated by the best translators in the world. So I hope you have learned a lot about these mysteries.

Select the texts that interest you the most and find out a little more about them because we should not stop seeking the truth about our origin.

Don't give up and keep finding out, reader.

Tablets 5, 6, and 7

Tablet 5

Le tus analyze the following text:
"After calculating how long the years lasted and when they died, he used the Nibiru terminal in order to give congruence to the stars."

According to Federico Lara Peinado, Nibiru is the nucleus through which all the luminous stars and enormous planets orbit. That is to say, everything revolved around Nibiru.

Nibiru is the bright North Star. Many researchers call it the Alpha Star of Cassiopeia. Nibiru is also linked to the giant planet Jupiter.

I have found many, many translations of Nibiru and I have found that they all agree on the same thing: Nibiru is the North Star that all other stars and planets revolve around. All planets and stars revolve around Nibiru. Other translations state that Nibiru is Mars. So what is Nibiru, is it the North Star, is it Jupiter, is it Mars?

For me, the translations of Federico Lara Peinado are the best translations because they are the most extensive. Federico Lara Peinado's translations have more details about all the myths and history of the Sumerians than any other translator.

So I trust Federico Lara Peinado more to state that Nibiru could be Jupiter.

But all translators agree on one thing: Nibiru is the North Star. We will analyze this in the following pages.

Let's read on:

"Near it he placed the terminals of the god Enlil and the god Ea, and opened immense gates on both sides of the immense and serene sky."

Nibiru being the central axis in the Celestial Vault, in the Universe, Marduk decided to give the ends of the Universe to Enlil and Ea.

It is important to me that you know that when I speak or question about Nibiru, you know that it is not a planet whose atmosphere needs gold to rebuild itself. No. Nibiru can be a North Star or Jupiter or Mars. This is said by the Sumerian tablets, Akkadian tablets, and Babylonian tablets. So Sitchin loses again. What he wrote are only fictional stories. Don't doubt that.

Let's read on:

"He placed a mountain over the head of the deceased mother of the gods Tiamat, and from that mountain a spring emerged. Many waves of water quaked, and from the eyes of Tiamat came forth the rivers that men would later call Euphrates and Tigris."

Here we can appreciate many things about the Mesopotamian culture and the later cultures that arose after this culture. We can also see the creation of the Tigris and Euphrates rivers.

I think the importance given to these two rivers is something that deserves to be highlighted by me because from the creation of the Tigris and Euphrates rivers, many cultures emerged. It is very interesting that they tell us that the beginning of creation was thanks to these two famous rivers.

Let's continue reading:

"The god Marduk gave the Tablet Me to Ea, this tablet he stole from Kingu. He gave it as a gift to Ea."

Here we see how the creation of humankind was prepared. Humankind is created with the blood of a traitor, the traitor Kingu. This is something that is not much discussed, but the tablets repeat this event over and over again in their texts.

In our veins runs the blood of Kingu, who was one of the supreme leaders of the goddess Tiamat, the goddess who died in the war against the Anunnaki.

The Me Tablets or Tablets of Destiny mean word, because with the word the Anunnaki gods could create or destroy anything they wanted.

As we discussed in previous chapters, the Me Tablets were devices that were inserted into the armor of the Anunnaki, making them the most powerful beings in the universe. Possession of the Me Tablets would make the holder the most powerful being in the universe. Perhaps the Me Tablets possessed some highly advanced technological mechanism or something similar, as they were considered the most powerful artifact that the Anunnaki possessed.

Let us continue reading:

"In old Babylon, which you mentioned, will be the place where your home will be for eternity."

This text indicates that Babylon is the temple of Marduk. According to the tablets, Babylon was built in heaven like a celestial palace floating in the sky.

Let us analyze the following text:

"Ea, the experienced one, practices the best methods in order to thus create his projects."

This text tells us that Ea is preparing the blood of Kingu in order to create humankind.

Tablet 6

Let us read the texts:

"I will solidify the blood and create strong bones. I will make a specimen whom everyone will call a young man, and he will be employed to serve and worship the gods, who will now be able to stop their labors."

"Kingu will be punished, his blood will be stolen, and with it, Ea will create the race of men."

"Ea will instruct the black-headed beings to worship the gods."

These texts narrate the creation of humankind. They also reveal how the gods created us and that, for them, we are only slaves who serve and worship them. We worship the gods because they are divine beings.

But, why do the gods need to be worshipped? Is it not enough to create and use human beings to do hard work? Several authors, including myself, think that there is a more advanced civilization than us, and they need our worship. The gods need to be worshipped because they love all the energies that arise when we pray, including our lower vibrations such as suffering, fear, and pain.

The "blackheads" mentioned in the text refer to human beings. The gods saw our hairy heads from the skies, from the heighs.

Tablet 7

Let's read the following text:

"Nibiru. It is he who sustains all the places of the universe and the constellations, also the sky and the earth. No one can go beyond his presence without consulting him. The star of great light, Nibiru, everyone can see him in the immense sky. He lives at the immense poles and all our gods behold him singing. He goes in and out of the bowels of Tiamat without tiring. His name forever will be Nibiru, he rules in the bowels of Tiamat, he arbitrates the course of the beautiful and shining stars of the great sky and illuminates the path of our lords gods, he is our shepherd".

Nibiru is one of the names of Marduk. Remember that Marduk had more than 50 names. Marduk loved the North Star Nibiru and called himself Nibiru.

Perhaps this metaphor means that the gods (the stars, constellations, and planets) were ruled and directed by Marduk (Nibiru). This makes more coherent sense, that Marduk was the center of all the gods. Marduk considered himself the center of the entire universe.

CONCLUSIONS

We must understand that everything that happens in the Enuma Elish, The Origin of Everything, is real. All the history described in the myth happened.

However, this is something dangerous because the Akkadians, who wrote the myth, did not witness these events. They did not exist during the creation of planet Earth or the arrival of the Anunnaki gods.

Instead, they inherited this tradition from the Sumerians and passed it down through their generations until their civilization disappeared.

It is likely that the Enuma Elish was modified over time, as the Akkadians adapted the Sumerian culture to their own. Therefore, the accuracy of the history described in the tablets may be questionable.

It is important to note that the Sumerians are older than the Akkadians and that the latter appropriated the former's culture after they disappeared.

Despite this, the Enuma Elish provides evidence of the Akkadians' effort to establish Marduk as the perfect and most powerful god. This led to the beginning of monotheism, which is the worship of only one god. Whether this actually happened or not is an interesting question to consider.

I believe that everything that the tablets say must be taken with caution, like a surgeon, because we need to approach them calmly in order to analyze and draw conclusions.

There are many authors who assert that the Enuma Elish represents something entirely different. According to these authors, the Enuma Elish simply portrays the collision between two celestial bodies that existed in the universe, namely Marduk and Tiamat.

This could be seen as a metaphor for what the Akkadians observed in the sky. They witnessed a cosmic catastrophe, and to them, it appeared as if gods were battling in the heavens.

Let us imagine that the Akkadians were able to witness a cosmic catastrophe, a collision between two planets, and for them, these colliding planets were seen as gods.

If this is true, then it is easy to speculate that the dialogues and names of the gods were merely inventions of the Akkadians, created to symbolize the ancient collision of two planets.

However, if such a collision did occur, would it have affected Earth in any way? Could this collision have caused the flood?

No one can confirm that. These questions are purely speculative in nature and rely on the interpretations of the authors.

But one thing we do know is that Marduk is associated with Mars, and Tiamat is associated with a planet that existed beyond Mars, possibly Phaethon, a hypothetical planet that might have been located in what is now known as the Asteroid Belt.

The hypothetical collision of these two planets

could have potentially created the Asteroid Belt beyond Mars.

Everything I mention is simply hypotheses that people often believe happened.

Another significant aspect concerning the Enuma Elish is Nibiru. Nibiru is only mentioned a couple of times in the Enuma Elish. It appears in the text on two occasions:

1. The first occurrence of Nibiru is when Marduk's name is mentioned: Nibiru. It is described as the central axis around which stars and planets revolve.

2. The second occurrence of Nibiru is when it is mentioned as being the North Star.

This seems important because there is no evidence of an elliptical orbit from a planet beyond Pluto. The notion of a mysterious planet that visits Earth every 3600 years is a fictional story, referred to as Nibiru or planet X. This hypothetical planet would be Nibiru, the planet of the Anunnaki.

Therefore, it can be concluded that this is another fictional story invented by Zecharia Sitchin. According to the tablets, there is no planet that approaches Earth every 3600 years.

Nibiru is also referred to as planet X.

So, I have demonstrated that Nibiru is not the planet where the Anunnaki supposedly lived. It is clear that Sitchin deceived us. However, we must acknowledge one thing: without his contributions, we might never have become aware of the Anunnaki. I enjoyed his fictional tales about the Anunnaki, and I must confess that I loved them. I don't mind that Sitchin lied to me; his stories were entertaining and inspired me to delve deeper into researching the Anunnaki, eventually leading me to write this book.

Remember: Sitchin is a writer of science fiction stories about the Anunnaki. The truth about the Anunnaki can be found in the Sumerian tablets, Akkadian tablets, and Babylonian tablets, which we all must decipher.

We only have to read what Zecharia Sitchin mentions in his fictional stories to understand that they are not found in the tablets. Nothing of what Sitchin told us in his books matches the tablets. The only thing that matches are the names of the most famous Anunnaki like Enki, Enlil, and Anu.

But I must admit that Sitchin was right about the existence of a planet. At present, there is a planet called Planet Nine that many scientists and astronomers are investigating. This Planet Nine is located beyond Pluto, and this coincides with Sitchin's fictional story.

The existence of Planet Nine coincides with some characteristics of Nibiru, but how is this possible?

The answer is easy. Zecharia Sitchin was very clever at inventing fictional stories. During his time, there were already rumors of the existence of a planet called Planet Nine. Many astronomers became obsessed with their searches, all wanting to find this famous Planet Nine.

However, what these scientists eventually found

was the planet Pluto. Zecharia Sitchin, being astute, seized the opportunity and said, *'I'm going to link Nibiru. Nibiru is a star, and I will link its name to the existence of a hypothetical planet, Planet Nine, that is located beyond Pluto. Since the discovery of the actual Planet Nine, it won't be too difficult to connect the names of this star, Nibiru, with that as yet unknown planet, Planet Nine'.*

The incredible thing about all this is that Sitchin was right; that planet did exist. However, during that time, astronomers considered it impossible, as their telescopes could only see Pluto, the most distant planet in the Solar System. Nonetheless, these astronomers had detected signs of a new planet beyond Pluto, though its existence remained a hypothesis, lacking certainty.

Seizing this opportunity, Zecharia Sitchin named this planet Number 9 and referred to it as Nibiru, the Planet Nibiru.

Now that you know the truth, whenever someone claims that Zecharia Sitchin speaks the truth about the Anunnaki, share with them what you have read in this book. Tell them that Zecharia Sitchin is an exceptional science fiction writer, but the true history lies within the Sumerian tablets, Akkadian tablets, and Babylonian tablets. Encourage them to read those translated tablets.

This book provides you, dear reader, with the necessary instructions to continue your quest for truth. Don't stop. The truth will set you free.

This book will set all of humankind free. Our

search has only just begun. May this book serve as the starting point for your new journey.

Reader, remember that absolute truth does not exist. Don't believe me, don't believe other authors, don't believe Sitchin and his fanatics, don't believe anyone.

My mission has already been accomplished, and I feel satisfied. My truth is derived from thorough analysis of the translations of the Sumerian tablets. I'm not sure if you agree with me, but I believe I have broadened your perspective and ignited your desire to learn more about the Anunnaki gods.

Embark on your journey, seek your own truth, and be liberated. It has been a pleasure guiding you, dear reader. Pursue the truth and embrace freedom!

AUTHOR'S NOTE

Everything you have read here, dear reader, is not an invention; it is the content of the Sumerian, Akkadian, and Babylonian tablets. They hold the absolute truth, so don't be fooled by anyone.

The most beautiful thing is that we have awakened from this dream. Our existence holds great value.

I believe our lives are immensely valuable because the gods depend on our negative emotions, positive emotions, and faith to sustain themselves. The only thing I know is that we must maintain a high vibration and frequency.

We must understand that myths hold hidden secrets for us. These myths should be studied in great detail. When we analyze a myth, such as the ones you have read in this book, I am aware that they conceal far more than my noble interpretation can comprehend. I genuinely feel insignificant, as the knowledge of the gods is infinite.

We are smaller than an atom in this vast universe; we are practically nothing.

Dear reader, you must study and respect the existing myths. They harbor countless secrets that deserve exploration.

Our ancestors witnessed many extraordinary deeds by these gods. They were unaware of the gods' technology, which is why they described their wars using terms familiar to their villages.

Chariots and horses in the sky, powerful winds, and lightning that rent the earth—these descriptions were their attempts to make sense of those supernatural phenomena they couldn't comprehend.

I remember the event where Moses, by stretching out his arms, opened the waters of the Red Sea. The waters parted, creating a pathway for God's Chosen People to walk through and escape.

What if Moses possessed advanced technology that enabled him to perform this miracle? Perhaps the staff he always carried in his hand was a technological device from the gods. I'm not certain about this, but it is a possibility.

I also remember Ezekiel, who was commanded by God to build a temple. God gave Ezekiel exact measurements for him to construct that temple, so that God could descend with His glory. God could descend from heaven onto a temple with specific, God-given measurements. This is engineering. However, what did God descend upon in the temple that Ezekiel built?

Various sacred texts document numerous historical events. Several cultures mention reptilian gods—beings with reptilian appearances such as snakes, dragons, and lizards. Some of these gods were benevolent towards us, while others sought our destruction. These gods fought amongst themselves to either save or annihilate us.

I remember how God commanded Abraham to sacrifice his firstborn, but when Abraham was determined to kill his son, an angel appeared and told him that enough was enough. The angel told Abraham to stop and reassured him that he should not kill his son because God had already proven His loyalty.

In other words, was God playing a tasteless joke, or was there another God who intervened to prevent such a horrific murder? The existence of multiple gods is unquestionable.

Now, do you understand why it is important to know, read, and interpret all these sacred and ancient texts?

Myths and ancient texts are necessary to discover the truth.

I believe you grasp the message, reader. Now it is your turn to investigate and find your own truth.

I hope you appreciate the surprise I have prepared for you on the last pages. You can download a free book about UFOs in the Bible. I hope you enjoy it. Sending you a warm hug, dear reader.

Paris, France
06/10/2020

THANK YOU!

Dear reader,

THANK YOU for choosing Anunnaki: Reptilians in the History of Humankind.

If you enjoyed the book, **a review would be appreciated** as it helps other readers discover this story.

If you want to know when my new books are released, you can sign up for my Reader's List and download a FREE BOOK here:

bit.ly/free-hkrane

(Write this in your browser, press enter, then you will be redirected to a registration page.)

I love you, reader.
I will see you in another story.
Henry Krane

CONTACT

Official Website (coming soon):
http://www.henrykrane.com

Email: **henry@henrykrane.com**

Facebook: **Henry Krane**

PRIVATE FACEBOOK GROUP:
bit.ly/group-hkrane

ABOUT THE AUTHOR

Henry Krane is an English science fiction and conspiracy writer. He was born in Liverpool, England, in 1981. He attended his first education at the José de San Martín National School. In 1991, he continued his studies at Cambridge Private School, where he discovered the stories of the writer Carl Sagan during his happy reading hours. Sagan became a great reference and inspiration for his writings, along with the writer David Icke.

Between 2000 and 2001, Henry dedicated himself to studying editorial design at the Institute of Graphic Design and Editorial Editons Soft. He consolidated his knowledge in the art of text layout and editing using different text editing programs.

In March 2004, he began his studies at the Institute of Computing and Informatics, Technical Institute of London, which he concluded in 2008. From that year onward, he devoted himself completely to writing. He started writing several stories in his personal blog but eventually deleted them based on the advice of his mentor.

Henry's stories focused on conspiracy and science fiction, genres that have fascinated him for as long as he can remember. While working as a web designer and desktop application programmer at LR Connection (LRC) since 2006, he continued writing passionately, exploring various genres such as Horror,

Drama, and Children's stories.

In October 2010, he decided to study Industrial Engineering at the University of Engineering, a profession that resonated with him. He absorbed a lot of knowledge about business and resumed working with his colleagues/partners at LRC. Together, they achieved internal improvements in the company, including better distribution of computer accessories to customers and improved employee satisfaction.

In 2012, Henry began working at a company specializing in Industrial Plastics as a Production Assistant. He continued in this role until 2017 when he became a Production Supervisor. However, during this time, he felt the calling to return to his true passion: writing.

With a business partnership and working in the new company, Henry decided to dedicate himself fully to literature. He currently has three books published in the most popular e-book retailers worldwide. These books are his first writings, consisting of short conspiracy stories. However, he has also written a trilogy that he hopes to finish soon for editing. Additionally, he has written a satellite book titled "ANUNNAKI" to provide background and understanding for his future books.

Henry's greatest desire in life is to continue contributing to the world of literature, and he has already begun doing so.

MORE BOOKS BY HENRY KRANE

Please visit this link:

bit.ly/hk-books

(Write the link in your browser, press enter, then you will be redirected to my official Facebook Group!)

DOWNLOAD A FREE BOOK!

If you want to know when my new books are released, you can sign up for my Reader's List and download a FREE BOOK here:

bit.ly/free-hkrane

(Write this in your browser, press enter, then you will be redirected to a registration page.)

I love you, reader.
I will see you in another story.
Henry Krane

RELATED BOOKS

-THE BOOK OF GAIA: Untold Mysteries and Secrets of the Universe, Urantia, and God

<u>bit.ly/the-book-of-gaia</u>

NOTE: If you have purchased the print version of this book, in order to purchase the books listed above, you must type the URL or link located under each title in your favorite internet browser, press the Enter key, and you will be redirected to the Amazon page ☺.

Please Leave a Review

Dear reader,

Thank you for your interest in my book.

Please, don't forget, if you enjoyed the book, **a review would be appreciated** as it helps other readers discover this story.

With love,
Henry Krane

Table of Contents

ANUNNAKI *REPTILIANS, HISTORY, MYTHS, SCIENCE AND HUMANKIND (2 BOOKS IN 1) BY HENRY KRANE*.......................... I

ANUNNAKI *REPTILIANS IN THE HISTORY OF HUMANKIND BY*.... I

THE REPTILE GODS 5

WE ARE REPTILIANS FOOD 10

DINOSAURS EXTINCTION AND THE WAR BETWEEN TWO RACES 17

THE CREATION OF THE GIANTS AND THE MAN 20

THE EXTINCTION OF ATLANTIS AND LEMURIA 25

THE TRUE ORIGIN OF THE MOON 34

THE BACKWARD EVOLUTION OF HUMANKIND 43

THE EXTINCTION OF PLANET MULGE 52

THE FINAL DECISION OF THE KADISTU 59

THE EXPULSION OF THE ANUNNAKI FROM URAS, EARTH 66

THE BIRTH OF THE MESSIAH 76

JESUS'S WAR DECLARATION TO ENLIL 88

THE GOD YAHWEH AND HIS NEW IDENTITY 96

THE PACT OF THE REPTILIAN BEINGS 104

ENLIL'S BIG FRAUD 112

THE ORIGIN OF THE JESUITS 119

THE ORIGIN OF ILLUMINATI	125
ENKI'S FIRST GREAT VICTORY	130
THE BEAUTIFUL DREAM OF TESLA	135
HITLER	140
THE CONSEQUENCES OF A BAD CHOICE	145
THE GREAT LIE OF THE ARRIVAL TO THE MOON	151
THE DESTINY OF THE HUMAN FARM	155
THE BEGINNING OF THE NEW WORLD ORDER	159
WE ARE THE ULTIMATE LIGHT	163
NOTE	170
ANUNNAKI *REPTILIANS BEYOND MYTH, SCIENCE AND HUMANKIND BY*	I
INTRODUCTION	175
AKKAD AND SUMER	177
THE MYTH OF CREATION	181
SUMERIAN TABLETS	186
AKKADIAN TABLETS	189
SUMERIAN UNIVERSAL FLOOD	192
ANUNNAKI IN SUMERIAN TABLETS	195
SUMERIAN SNAKES	206
THE TABLETS OF DESTINY	209
THE SEVEN SAGES	211

MESOPOTAMIA	218
MORE MYHTS	220
SUMERIAN PEOPLE	225
MYTHS OF HEROES AND DEMONS	228
THE MYTH OF THE AFTERLIFE	242
THE CREATION OF EVERYTHING	253
MORE SACRED TEXTS	263
MORE TRANSLATED TEXTS	273
TABLETS 5, 6, AND 7	279
CONCLUSIONS	284
AUTHOR'S NOTE	290
THANK YOU!	293
CONTACT	294
ABOUT THE AUTHOR	295
MORE BOOKS BY HENRY KRANE	297
DOWNLOAD A FREE BOOK!	298
RELATED BOOKS	299
PLEASE LEAVE A REVIEW	300

Made in United States
North Haven, CT
11 January 2025

64336481R00166